THY KINGDOM COME:
The Fight for America

Dr. Michelle A. Morrison

Books can be purchased from:
www.amazon.com
www.barnesandnoble.com
publisher link: store.virtualbookworm.com
author link: www.thronerm.com

All scriptures taken from the King James Version of the Bible, unless noted otherwise.

"Thy Kingdom Come: *The Fight for America*," by Dr. Michelle A. Morrison. ISBN 978-1-62137-014-7.

Published 2012 by Virtualbookworm.com Publishing Inc., P.O. Box 9949, College Station, TX 77842, US. ©2012, Dr. Michelle A. Morrison. All rights reserved. No part of this publication may be reproduced, stored in a retrieval system, or transmitted in any form or by any means, electronic, mechanical, recording or otherwise, without the prior written permission of Dr. Michelle A. Morrison.

Manufactured in the United States of America.

Dedication

First, I dedicate this book to the sweet, precious Holy Spirit. I am thankful for the times You refreshed me, revived me, gave me hope, and drew me unto Yourself.

Second, I am eternally grateful to, and honor the strong Proverbs 31 women who influenced my life – my beloved mother, Mavis Jacobs, who sacrificed her life for her eight children, and my cherished late grandmother Ida Rowe, whose memory lives on with me forever.

Author's Online Store:

Visit: www.thronerm.com
Throne Room, Incorporated
Or contact author at PO Box 1338, New York,
N.Y. 10008-1338

Follow the author on Twitter at:
https://twitter.com/drmmorrison

Contents

Introduction

It is my position in this book that the United States of America is a Christian nation. In God we trust. The Ten Commandments are still displayed prominently behind our US Supreme Court Justices when they take the bench. Much evidence in our history points to hope in the Judeo-Christian God. It was prayer that won America independence from Great Britain in the Revolutionary War of the 1700s, as we will see later.

Despite arguments to the contrary, this book will prove our Christian foundation. An 1892 United States Supreme Court decision (which we will examine in Chapter 1) formally concluded that we are a Christian nation. The holding in that 1892 case regarding our Christian world status cannot be denied. Many have successfully disputed and uprooted some of the laws and religious emblems in our culture that demonstrate our Christian heritage.

However, there are so many other legal and token evidence which show that we are a Christian republic. A majority of Americans claim to be Christian, even if some do not practice the faith.

To be fair to both liberal and conservative points of view regarding the issue of our Christian origin or present status, we will later closely examine what I mean by "Christian nation." Much of the debate over this issue can be solved by first looking at this crucial definition. Once that is given, then people may not agree with the definition, but most certainly cannot debate the evidence presented in support thereof.

This book attempts to present a fair analysis of this topic. I never want to be accused of twisting facts to support a religious point of view. While I do believe that we are a Christian country, this does not mean that pagan or anti-Christian religious ideals did not affect some people and practices from our nation's inception, or that religion was meant to control the government of the United States. I certainly acknowledge anti-Christian influences; but I believe we must identify those pagan beliefs and emblems, repent before God as a nation, and do everything within our power to maintain the Christian values held by the majority of Americans from the start.

It is undeniable that the moral standards originally implemented into our laws were based on Christian principles. It is also undeniable that we have digressed tremendously from some of these

Christian precepts. As a result, the enemy has gained access to harm our country. To be clear, I believe Satan launched a spiritual war for the soul of America from the very beginning through pagan Enlightenment philosophies, which we will examine later. But I will present evidence to those who stop there, that through revival and awakening fires, the Lord also powerfully intervened on our behalf from the outset.

Therefore, I will argue that from the birth of this republic, there has been a conflict between opposing forces of a good God and the evil deceiver, Satan. When we stray further and further away from Christian values, we lose the war. When we come back to God, He is merciful and helps us. We are now in a dark time where America and the world are being rocked by one catastrophe after another. We can turn it all around and win the fight by allowing God to draw us back unto Himself.

The title of this book is deceptive, unless we understand Christianity's definition of "fighting," "war," and "battle." All of these terms simply mean "prayer unto God." Yes, there is a peaceful way to win the war for America – a peaceful way to defeat terrorism and all other attacks on this great country.

There is currently a spiritual battle ensuing for the economic world status and for the very soul of

America. I continue to label it a "spiritual battle" because a dear friend of mine, upon hearing the title of this book, misunderstood the meaning of "fight" and stated, "Why is it that there is always a war in religion?"

I immediately explained that Jesus never advocated for physical violence. The war I speak of is a "spiritual," non-violent war. There are times when a country must defend itself (physical war), but that is not the kind of war I am referring to. The fight I speak of is only through falling on our knees in humility and prayer.

The terrorist attacks on our country resulted from Satan's war against this nation. We can only ultimately win this spiritual battle though faith in Jesus Christ. The Bible tells us that we are in a fight, but that we war not against flesh and blood. Instead, we war against spiritual forces of darkness, or wickedness in high places (Eph. 6:12). The scriptures go on to tell us that we can engage the enemy and win with non-violent weapons such as putting on the "breastplate of righteousness" and "praying always" (Eph. 6:14, 18).

The precious Holy Spirit, through Divine favor, revealed to me the truths contained in this book. All of the credit goes to Him. As I conducted my research, the Holy Spirit began to show me that Satan has often fooled and ensnared us throughout this nation's history. My non-Christian friend once told me a saying he deemed a joke, which is that "the biggest trick Satan has played on us is to convince us that he (Satan) is not real." This is far from a joke—it is stark reality. Satan was a deceiver from the start, and he is called, in the Bible, the father of lies. We must corporately repent and turn back to God with prayer and fasting. It is only He who can turn our economy around and save us.

The statements that follow may very well be the most important comments made in this entire book.

I want to make it emphatically clear upfront that this book was not written to point the finger at the unsaved in condemnation. Jesus told the religious leaders, concerning the woman caught in adultery, that the only one who can judge is that one without sin. Only Jesus Christ lived a spotless life. The Bible tells us that we have all sinned and fallen short of the glory of God (Rom. 3:23). The apostle Paul noted that of all the sinners, he had been the chief (I Tim. 1:15).

I certainly can identify with Paul's statement. Even after being in ministry for a few years, the Lord had to deliver me from many sinful ways that were not pleasing in His sight. At one point I had felt so "holier than thou," until the Lord showed me areas of sin in my own life that I had denied or overlooked. He wanted to deal with those areas. As recently as 2008, He placed me in a wilderness or dry place, where I had to come to terms with hidden anger, bitterness, hatred and resentment that were buried in my own heart. The Lord set me on a journey to close the doors to areas of sin in my life and to get to know Him more intimately. I separated from family and friends for several years, in my quest to really experience a true heart transformation.

I am going to now make a bold but true statement. Although we do have many sincere believers in the Body of Christ, many have never been truly or fully converted. Some individuals attend church out of habit. People are amazed that leaders fall; but the truth is, we are just human like everyone else. And yes, God holds us to a higher standard; but if we reach a place where we are not spending time with God and not separating from the world, sin will enter.

The Bible tells us that we must die daily to sin (1Cor. 15:31). This verse is simply an admonition for us all, both saved and unsaved, to repent individually and corporately. It is God Himself who sets about to do a work in us if we let Him. Only Jesus Christ is perfect, but until we are taken from these mortal and sinful bodies, the key is to truthfully recognize areas where our lives may be in violation of His statutes. We must then repent and refuse to live in a place of habitual sin. And if we fall, we should quickly ask for God's forgiveness, make a change, and do not live in condemnation.

Again, this book was written after a time period where God dealt with my own denied areas of sin. I cannot therefore come before you to condemn. I can only tell you that God loves us. He loves America and has fought for this country from the very beginning, in response to the prayers of a majority population. I can come before you openly because I have died to "self." I sincerely cried out to the Lord for a true conversion experience, and He answered my cry.

My sister recently shared with me a story about her daughter. Because she hadn't seen me in a while, my little niece went to her mom, crying and proclaiming that Auntie Chelle was dead. When my sister called me, concerned, I thought to myself, "Out of the mouth of babes." I can honestly say that for the first time in my Christian walk, I feel a true death to "self." He said that if we search for Him with all of our hearts, we will find Him. I will never say that I am perfect, but I come before you in humility – a laid down lover advocating the cause of Jesus. He has answered my cry and changed me from the inside out.

Although secularly I am an attorney at law, the Lord told me to present the evidence in this book to America that He won the battle for this country from the start, and that He wants to intervene again on our behalf. I have included numerous historical references, lest it be said that the writer has made up the facts to support her argument.

I write this book with tears in my eyes. I write this book with fire in my soul – a fire that cannot be quenched, but must burn so that the world can see that Jesus Christ is Lord of America. I write this book to not only show the stark reality of the darkness that covers the earth, but also to show the graciousness of a loving God. His ways are far above our understanding.

As an attorney, I am all too familiar with the reasoning of the intellectual spirit. We must have a logical answer in order to believe. This "ever-reasoning mind" fooled some during the Enlightenment age, as we will later see. Unfortunately, those who tend to focus only on logic often have a hard time exercising faith, which is the basis of Christianity. We must come to God by faith.

I am passionate because I have come to know Him not only as Savior, but as Friend. He has proven Himself to me on so many occasions. I have seen Him heal so many terminally ill people in my ministry. I have also seen Him provide jobs and work other miracles.

There is none righteous, no, not one. We are saved by faith in Jesus Christ, not by our "goodness," lest anyone should boast (Eph. 2:8-9).

I appeal to you as a fellow citizen and friend. Let God's grace have its work in your heart. Pray that that the Lord reveals to you the truths written in this book.

God's Grace Abounds

One thing the Holy Spirit laid heavily on my heart while writing this book is that it is important for people to know about God's tremendous love and mercy. He is a God of grace and has been so faithful to America over the centuries. The Lord has given us many opportunities to change our ways and come to Him. Even now, in the midst of these times of crises, if we repent, pray and ask for forgiveness, He is sure to hear our cry and help us.

There are presently so many catastrophes affecting our nation and the world. And there is still so much more to come if we do not change. In 2011, a congresswoman stated that God was trying to get our attention through hurricanes and earthquakes. In addition, I recently saw an article online where a preacher warned people that the crack in the Washington monument after the 2011 earthquake was a sign of God's judgment.

I then read many statements from unbelievers in response. Some of these comments pointed out that churches had been destroyed through catastrophes as well. One person even mentioned that Christians in Texas had recently prayed for rain, but that Texas had continued to experience the worst drought in *over a century*. The unbelievers wanted to know if God's judgment was also upon the Church.

I wanted to answer back in the affirmative regarding the question of whether God would judge the Church. God has shaken and continues to shake the Church. The Bible tells us that judgment first starts in the house of God. But Christians make the right move in calling a time of fasting and prayer; this is the only way we will see God's forgiveness, protection and blessing in these dark times. If we come to Him in true humility and prayer, He will hear us and heal our land.

We must constantly pray for our leaders. Christians vote based on issues that do not break God's statutes. Regardless of whom the Lord allows in any office, the Bible admonishes us to pray for all leaders, so that there is peace in the land. We may not always agree with every decision in government, but we have to pray for these leaders nonetheless. The fate of the country rests in their hands. Therefore, we need God to influence them.

I believe that He will continue to raise up Godly men and women to govern key areas of our country, and I pray that the fires of revival will radically touch the hearts of all (regardless of party), so that others in government and American society can see the need for God in these dark times.

Chapter 1: Is America a Christian Nation?

In 1905, US Supreme Court Justice David Brewer defined what constitutes a Christian nation, and I completely agree with that definition. He stated:

> We classify nations in various ways. As, for instance, by their form of government. One is a kingdom, another an empire, and still another a republic. Also by race. Great Britain is an Anglo-Saxon nation, France a Gallic, Germany a Teutonic, Russia a Slav. And still again by religion. One is a Mohammedan nation, others are heathen, and still others are Christian nations.
>
> This republic is classified among the Christian nations of the world. *It was so formally declared by the Supreme Court of the United States.* In the case of Holy Trinity Church *v*. United States, 143 U. S. 471, that court, after mentioning various circumstances, added, "[T]hese and many other matters which might be noticed, add a volume of unofficial declarations to the

mass of organic utterances that this is a Christian nation."

But in what sense can it be called a Christian nation? Not in the sense that Christianity is the established religion or that the people are in any manner compelled to support it. On the contrary, the Constitution specifically provides that "Congress shall make no law respecting an establishment of religion, or prohibiting the free exercise thereof." Neither is it Christian in the sense that all its citizens are either in fact or name Christians. On the contrary, all religions have free scope within our borders. Numbers of our people profess other religions, and many reject all. Nor is it Christian in the sense that a profession of Christianity is a condition of holding office or otherwise engaging in the public service, or essential to recognition either politically or socially. In fact the government as a legal organization is independent of all religions.

Nevertheless, *we constantly speak of this republic as a Christian nation* – in fact, as the leading Christian nation of the world.[1]

Justice Brewer therefore cited the landmark 1892 case of *Church of the Holy Trinity v. United*

States, which formally concluded that this republic is a Christian nation.

Based on Brewer's definition above, a Christian nation is not determined by the issue of the Establishment Clause's requirement of "separation of Church and State." We will examine later specifically what that legal concept means, and why it was implemented by the forefathers.

A Christian nation, then, is first and foremost a nation where the majority people, from its inception, believed themselves to be Christian. There is no requirement that 1) Christianity be the governmentally established religion, 2) the State mandate the population to support Christianity, or 3) those who hold public offices be qualified only if they are Christian.

If we look at a nation such as China, for example, we may call that nation, for the most part, a Buddhist nation. We would form that conclusion not because the laws require people to worship Buddha, but because Buddhism is the religion of the majority. Christians comprise only a very small percentage of the population in China. The Chinese government technically allows freedom of religion (Constitution of 1982), but it is clear that the nation is not Christian because Christianity is practiced by only a very small percentage. It is a well-known fact that Christians have been persecuted tremendously in China over the centuries.

In the same way, Islam is the majority religion in Iraq, with a very small percentage of Christians. Iraq's constitution recognizes Islam as the official religion, but it also calls for freedom of religious belief. Again, it is a well-known fact that Christians have been tremendously persecuted in Iraq.

So clearly we see that a country can create laws giving religious freedom, but the religion of the majority, as well as the laws and tolerance of that country for other religions, often determine how we categorize the overall religion of a particular nation.

I would argue that the standard for determining the religion of a nation is not solely based upon whether that country "officially" recognizes a particular religion as the nation's faith, although that can certainly be a determinative factor.

A particular nation can also rightfully be said to be of a particular religion where the entire political, socioeconomic, governmental, and legal systems that govern the people were derived originally from the principles of that particular faith. Justice Brewer's analysis further supports this view, where he noted that Christianity shaped and molded America. The wonderful thing about his analysis is that he looked back to the very beginning, even before the drafting of the Declaration of Independence. He mentioned that the people established this Christian foundation from the first settlement on our shores.

I fully accept Justice Brewer's definition, despite any anti-Christian influences that crept in at the country's inception. I believe God honored the actions of a true Christian majority who undeniably implemented Christian tenets throughout the socioeconomic and governmental systems of America. The Lord would not ignore the cry of the people to serve Him, even where paganism affected some people and leaders, or may have affected some practices from the start.

Justice Brewer cited the commission from "Ferdinand and Isabella to Columbus," hoping that God would assist with the new discovery.[2] He noted that the first colonial grant in 1584 authorized Sir Walter Raleigh to enact government statutes, as long as they were not against the Christian faith.[3] He mentioned the charter of New England (1620) and Massachusetts (1629) respectively, which contained language about advancing the Christian religion and obeying the Christian faith.[4] The 1777 constitution of Vermont granted the free exercise of religious worship, but noted that people should observe the Sabbath or the Lord's day.[5] In these early beginnings, several colonies and states even made the Christian faith a requirement to hold office.[6]

Brewer thus used the many declarations originally contained in charters, statutes and constitutions to prove his point. He made a noteworthy observation that in none of these items were Mohammed, Confucius or Buddha mentioned.[7] In making that statement, there was no disrespect intended against other religions; Brewer simply presented the facts to support his arguments concerning our unquestionable Christian foundation.

If we look more closely at the text of the 1892 decision of *Holy Trinity*, Justice Brewer affirmed that we are a Christian nation because the entire population voiced this belief, and Christianity was a part of the common law:

> They speak the voice of the entire people...in *Updegraph v. Commonwealth,* 11 S. & R. 394, 400, it was decided that "Christianity, general Christianity, is, and always has been, a part of the common law of Pennsylvania;...not Christianity with an established church and tithes and spiritual courts, but Christianity with liberty of conscience to all men."

> And in *People v. Ruggles,* 8 Johns. 290, 294-295, Chancellor Kent, the great

commentator on American law, speaking
as Chief Justice of the Supreme Court of
New York, said:

"The people of this state, in common with
the people of this country, *profess the
general doctrines of Christianity as the
rule of their faith* and practice...[8]

If there is any legal case that attempts to reverse the
powerful conclusions made by Justice Brewer in
Holy Trinity, that decision would have to cite just as
compelling evidence to support the proposition that
we are no longer a Christian republic. If such
evidence is not presented, I would emphatically
conclude that Brewer's analysis *still stands* as truth
in the never ending debate on this topic.

Until we strip this country of all of the laws,
emblems and majority Christian claims of the
people, I would deem as weak any attempt to
contradict Brewer's holding. I am not saying here
that Satan has not influenced some to remove
many laws and symbols of Christianity. But I
would conclude that as of the writing of this book,
we have enough remaining proof (as I will show)
that we are still "Christian" under Brewer's
definition.

Two recent cases which acknowledged our
Christian heritage are: *Marsh v. Chambers*, 463
U.S. 783 (1983) (United States Supreme Court
upheld government funding for chaplains to open

legislative sessions with prayer as constitutional because of the "unique history" of the US) and *Lynch v. Donnelly*, 465 U.S. 668 (1984) (United States Supreme Court upheld the legality of Christmas holiday decorations on town property).

In the 1983 *Marsh* case, the court concluded that the Nebraska legislature's practice of opening sessions with religious prayer (by a Presbyterian chaplain) did not violate the Establishment Clause. The court noted that the very first Congress paid a chaplain even while preparing to adopt the Establishment Clause! The court also commented that this practice has gone uninterrupted for over 200 years, and is a part of the fabric of our society.

In reading and comparing later United States Supreme Court cases to earlier cases regarding Christianity, it is evident that in more recent cases, the court relied on "tradition" to support upholding Christian practices. In earlier rulings such as *Holy Trinity*, the court blatantly concluded that we are a Christian nation.

Although I believe that we have erred in not continuing to *directly* affirm this nation as Christian, I believe it is extremely significant that 1) the United States Supreme Court has upheld a Christian chaplain opening up legislative sessions as part of our heritage, and 2) the ruling in *Holy Trinity* that this nation is Christian has not been formally or *clearly* reversed (although this was technically not the main issue of the case). I have not found any legal case which presents compelling evidence to support a proposition that we are no longer a Christian nation.

I believe that this is significant not only in the natural, but also in the spiritual – it is important to God. I believe that the *Marsh* and *Holy Trinity* cases can be used to effectively argue before the throne room of heaven that we are a Christian country. This will help to ease the wrath of God as many in our culture try to shut Him out.

And although we have ruled to take prayer out of schools, clearly we still uphold practices such as hiring Christian chaplains to open legislative sessions with prayer. In addition, a majority of the population still profess Christianity, as I have stated. Most importantly, the Lord will hear the prayer of the Church – the Body of Christ. We have been crying out to Him for mercy, and for revival to hit this land.

I want to add here that 1) there is artwork exhibited on the capitol building where the US Supreme Court is located; there are displays of the world's lawgivers, and all other pieces are facing one in the center – an emblem of Moses with the Ten Commandments, 2) two large oak doors leading into the actual US Supreme Court courtroom contain etchings of the Ten Commandments, 3) the wall right above the US

Supreme Court Justices exhibits a picture of the Ten Commandments, and 4) there are numerous bible verses etched in stone throughout federal buildings and upon federal monuments in Washington DC. All of these symbols prove our Christian foundation.

I read online that one pastor was dismayed when he took a tour of the US Supreme Court building and the tour-guide failed to talk about the displays of Moses with the Ten Commandments. After conducting research, the pastor allegedly found out that references to the Ten Commandments had been purposefully omitted! I cannot confirm the veracity of this finding. But folks, if this is indeed true, I stress that, as the Church, we are sitting back while atheists try to remove proof of our heritage. In the same way other etchings are discussed from a historical context, why would it violate the Establishment Clause to teach the public about our religious foundation? We must not be silent as these injustices occur.

In a time when the enemy would like to strip away every proof of a Christian heritage, we must fight to keep what remains. One way to do this is to file lawsuits with the US Supreme Court (and all other courts where applicable) to reverse decisions that are contrary to the early cases establishing our Christian roots and status. The Bible admonishes that Christians should not sue each other, but this does not apply to protecting our legal rights when the enemy attacks.

John Adams, the first vice president of the United States (1789-1797), and the second president (1797–1801), stated:

> The GENERAL PRINCIPLES on which the fathers achieved independence, were ... the general principles of Christianity, in which all those sects were united...

> Now I will avow that I then believed, and now believe, that those general principles of Christianity are as eternal and immutable as the existence and attributes of God; and that those principles of liberty are as unalterable as human nature, and our terrestrial mundane system.[9]

In fact, history reveals that most of our past presidents claimed to be Christian.

In his 2006 book entitled *Faith and the Presidency: From George Washington to George W. Bush*, Gary Scott Smith commented that religion and politics have been very much woven into all of America's history.[10] He highlighted that even from the beginning, the Pilgrims and all others in our history thought this nation was chosen by God, with a "divine mission to promote freedom, peace, and justice in the world and serve as a haven for the persecuted and oppressed and a land of opportunity for the ambitious and devout."[11]

Reformers, ministers, businessmen and presidents alike have felt America embodied democracy, freedom and morality. Jefferson called this country "the last best hope of mankind."[12] Theodore Roosevelt felt our welfare was connected to that of humanity in general. Smith noted that politicians have always based their policies on ideals grounded in religion. He quoted G. K. Chesterton as naming America "the nation with the soul of a church."[13]

All of our presidents welcomed organized religion; thirty two of them were church members.[14] Smith commented that in every presidential inaugural address, with the exception of President Washington's short second speech, these leaders asked for God's blessing on the country.[15] In addition, despite the issue of separation of Church and State, over the years, Congressional sessions still open with prayer, we still appoint chaplains in the military, our coins still declare trust in God, and our presidents still call for national days of prayer.[16]

Whether some of our past presidents were influenced by other religions at different points in their careers is another issue altogether. The important fact in this section is that most of them openly confessed or adhered to Christian tenets. I would add that our current president, Barack Obama (who is the first African-American president), has stated that he is Christian. The goal in this section is to simply show the Christian roots of the vast majority of our presidents.

Some other factors that prove our Christian heritage are: our national anthem in its full wording mentions trust in God; the Thanksgiving holiday was instituted to give thanks to God; the famous Liberty Bell, which signifies American independence, carries the inscription of Leviticus 25:10 (proclaiming liberty throughout the land); and the Pledge of Allegiance mentions our nation being "under God." I mention other proofs throughout the book.

In addition, America is still a professed majority Christian population. A 2004 ABC News poll stated:

> Eighty-three percent of Americans identify themselves as Christians. Most of the rest, 13 percent, have no religion. That leaves just 4 percent as adherents of all non-Christian religions combined — Jews, Muslims, Buddhists and a smattering of individual mentions.[17]

If we still are not convinced, I present further evidence throughout this book as to why we are a Christian republic under Justice Brewer's definition. However, at this time I will address several arguments made by those who disagree.

1. Separation of Church and State

The US Constitution (art. 6, sec. 3) forbids a religious test as a requirement to hold public office. The First Amendment states that "Congress shall make no law respecting an establishment of religion, or prohibiting the free exercise thereof..." (US Const., amend. I).

One of the most misunderstood legal principles is that of "separation of Church and State" in the Establishment Clause, as cited above. The forefathers wanted to keep the Church from *directing* the legal and governmental systems of the nation because of the harm that can come from religious control. However, as we have seen from our numerous previous examples, the majority of the people were still Christian, and the entire socioeconomic system of the country centered around Christian principles.

This is why we can have separation of Church and State, and yet have "In God We Trust" as our motto. It was our Christian values that led us to fight to obtain freedom for all. The problem is that we have come to the place where we erroneously focus only on "freedom," and have left behind the God who won us that liberty.

Separation of Church and State is therefore not incompatible with the notion that we are a Christian country.

In the 1811 case, *People v. Ruggles,* which was cited by Justice Brewer, James Kent, New York Chief Justice, opined:

> The object of the 38th article of the constitution, was, to "guard against spiritual oppression and intolerance," by declaring that "the free exercise and enjoyment of religious profession and worship, without discrimination or preference, should for ever thereafter be allowed within this state, to all mankind." This declaration[,] (noble and magnanimous as it is, when duly understood[,]) never meant to withdraw religion in general...Christianity, in its enlarged sense, as a religion revealed and taught in the Bible, is not unknown to our law. The *statute for preventing immorality (Laws, vol. 1. 224. R. S. 675, s. 69, e t seq.)* consecrates the first day of the week[,] as holy time, and considers the violation of it as immoral. This was only the continuation, in substance, of a law of the colony which declared[,] that the profanation of the Lord's day was "the great scandal of the Christian faith."[18]

A very important legal principle when examining statutes and case law is that of "original intent." This simply means that we must examine the "intent" of the framers of a statute, or the court that establishes precedent, when interpreting that rule or decision. We see that Justice Kent in *People v. Ruggles* correctly explained that the "intent" of separation of Church and State was to protect from religious intolerance, not to remove Christianity, which the case defended.

If we look at the history of so many countries and the ills that have been done to support a particular religion, it becomes clear why the founding fathers of the United States wanted to ensure that religion did not control the State. It was their Christian values, I believe, that led them to try to protect the interests of the people. In addition, God gave us all free will and forces Himself on none. Therefore, giving people freedom to choose their faith is not incompatible with God giving us free will.

The critical issue is that the Christian religion must remain prominent, with its values continuing to influence our social, economic, legal and government systems.

The problem is, with misunderstanding of the interpretation of "separation of Church and State," over the years many have tried to uproot the clear Christian values that are evidenced throughout the land. Keeping "In God We Trust" as our official motto, "One Nation Under God" as a part of our Pledge of Allegiance, or keeping the Ten Commandments displayed in our US Supreme Court building, does not mean that we are making laws establishing a religion. Simply put, they are powerful proofs of our heritage and Christian foundation.

2. Enlightenment Influence

In order to understand the Enlightenment period in history and its impact on the United States, we must look in depth at the Protestant Reformation (1517–1648). The Renaissance period in history had led to excessive sales of indulgences (remissions of punishment due to sin), and other ills in the Catholic Church. A German theologian named Martin Luther publicly challenged these types of practices, and this resulted in what is called the Protestant Reformation in Europe. Luther published *The Ninety-Five Theses* in 1517 and attempted to reform what he believed to be the Catholic Church's corruption and false beliefs, including teachings on purchasing indulgences and the sale of clerical offices.

Devastating and bloody wars resulted in Europe from the Protestant Reformation as Catholic and Protestant fought each other. Christianity was greatly divided. [19] Thus, anti-Christian mindsets developed.[20] When the Reformation ended in 1648, philosophers started to re-evaluate the belief

17

system. The Enlightenment Age, or Age of Reason, was a period during the 17th and 18th centuries where the intellectuals of the time tried to reform beliefs in society through reason.

This was, in essence, a scientific revolution where great philosophers rejected religion and embraced humanistic faith, or faith through knowledge and reason. The prior Medieval and Reformation eras had been grounded in Christian beliefs. These new thinkers turned away from Christian doctrine. Empiricists in Britain explained the world based on the senses, and Rationalists in France and Germany looked at everything from the standpoint of reason only. John Locke, David Hume and George Berkeley were Empiricists in the forefront, while Baruch Spinoza and Rene Descartes led the Rationalists.

Hume introduced skepticism, which led many to doubt the supernatural aspect of Christianity. Rationalists like Immanuel Kant merged Empiricism with Rationalism and concluded that God's existence could not be proven. Christians began both schools of thought. Locke, Berkeley, and Descartes were believers, but other notables created theories that were completely anti-Christian.[21]

Deism is an Enlightenment religious and philosophical belief based on reason, which influenced some during that period. Deists generally believe that a supreme being created the universe, but that this god does not intervene in human affairs. They teach that this distant god made the universe, but wants the main focus to be on the laws he established for the independent operation of the world.

Locke was a Christian and Deist. Isaac Newton, the famous intellect who greatly impacted the comprehension of mathematics and science, was Deist. He believed that Jesus was sent as a "redeemer" to save mankind, but rejected Christ's Divinity.[22] The wealthy elites of the mid-eighteenth century followed the new philosophical trend. Both Catholics and Protestants tried to defend Christianity, which was under great attack. Enlightenment thinking resulted in people leaving the Church.[23]

Enlightenment Freemasonry also influenced some from the 17th century onward. Over previous centuries, certain guilds or lodges in Europe would oversee workers such as carpenters, bell makers, surgeons, or masons. Benefits of membership in these guilds included wage protection and social life. During the 17th century, the lodges started to accept non-Masons as members, mostly because of the need for dues. These organizations may have appealed to educated non-Masons because of stories about the antiquity of the lodges.

It is unclear how the guilds changed from a membership of workers to a society for men.

However, Freemasonry developed into a ritualistic, hierarchical and secret society. One historian saw Scotland as the basis of 17th century Freemasonry, but much of it reflected the ideology of Britain's uprising against royal power.[24]

Masonic teaching included topics such as equality for all men, brothers becoming enlightened philosophers, advancing through merit, and civic virtue.[25] Masons welcomed the religions of the members' countries, which could range from theism to atheism.[26] Lodges rarely had openly Christian tenets, and the Catholic Church condemned Freemasonry as a cult in 1738.

The condemnation by the Church made the lodges even more appealing to the secular mind. The wealthy began governing themselves in these organizations. Membership symbolized maturity in politics and separation from Church authority, as well as drinking and fun. The lodges spread as far west as Philadelphia, and even to Haiti.[27]

Some believe that George Washington and other founding fathers were Freemasons.

The people who fled from Britain to the new land that now comprises the US, were people who had seen the ills done in the name of government-controlled religion. Most of the first colonists were Protestants and wanted the Church separate from the State. Although a majority of the colonists were Christians, Deism and other Enlightenment ideologies influenced some of the people, as well as some of the forefathers such as Benjamin Franklin and Thomas Jefferson.[28] However, during this same time (see Chapter 3 for more detail), certain evangelists would emerge and lead revivals that would shake the world.[29]

Some would argue that the Declaration of Independence (US 1776) refers to "the god of Nature" because of Enlightenment influence. I will say here that Christians have also interpreted that statement to mean the God of Christianity. Others would prefer to completely ignore any references to God. Whether that statement refers to the Deist god or our Christian God, only the framers knew. An argument may be made for both Christians and Deists in this regard.

I want to make a powerful point here that although a few of the founding fathers may have been influenced at some point by Deism, Freemasonry, or other similar ideologies, many of their statements show that they were indeed Christian gentlemen at certain points in their careers, with Christian values much like the larger American population and governing structure around them. Some may have never released their Christian foundation while embracing other ideologies. We see in Chapter 2 that Franklin most likely changed his Deist thinking toward the end of his life and embraced Christianity.

The Bible does tell us that we should serve no other gods; Jesus Christ is the only way to salvation. So to the extent that at different time periods our founding fathers were influenced by Enlightenment thinking, the Bible teaches that God would judge those sins. To the extent that such thinking affected any area of our culture, God would judge the nation. But I want to clarify that we cannot erase their Christian statements, as much as we cannot ignore the fact that they may have been impacted by pagan thinking at some points in time.

The key here is that the majority of the American population were sincere Christians. Other key leaders such as Patrick Henry, John Jay and Alexander Hamilton were staunch Christians.[30]

Therefore, we cannot let the Enlightenment influence on some, lead to the conclusion that this is not a Christian nation, that God did not bless us, or that He forever damned America. I firmly believe that the voice of a majority Christian nation has spoken powerfully to our God over the centuries. That voice has tremendously impacted the Lord, who would not destroy a land where most of its inhabitants called on His name.

The problem is, anti-Christian thought permeated from the beginning, thus indicating that Satan subtly deceived some of the American Christian population into straying away from God. In the same way, the serpent beguiled Eve and Adam. But the majority still upheld God's statutes.

In modern-day US, the serpent continues to beguile. The only difference is that, unlike the majority population at the nation's inception, many in this current majority Christian population *do not* follow Christian principles. The serpent's mark has really set in: this is why, although over 80% of Americans currently proclaim themselves Christians, many would say, "Has God really said there is life at conception?" Other so-called Christians lobby to remove Christian emblems and traditions in an attempt to "promote religious freedom." We have forgotten that "religious freedom" was never meant to remove proof of our heritage, or to violate God's laws. We must reclaim ground by turning back to our Savior.

3. Treaty of Tripoli

Article 11 of the Treaty of Tripoli (a peace treaty between the US and the Muslim nation of Tripolitania to prevent piracy against American ships in the Mediterranean sea), which was ratified by the US Senate in 1797, states, "As the Government of the United States of America is not, in any sense, founded on the Christian religion; as it has in itself no character of enmity against the laws, religion, or tranquility [sic], of Mussulmen [Muslims]; and, as the said States never have entered into any war, or act of hostility against any Mahometan nation, it is declared by the parties, that no pretext arising from religious opinions, shall ever produce an interruption of the harmony existing between the two countries."

Some cite this treaty to support the theory that we are not a Christian nation. Others claim that Christians want to ignore the treaty. I do not want to ignore this treaty. I do not believe it contradicts the points I have been making. But again, I would go back to Justice Brewer's definition of a Christian nation. I say this because 1) the original colonists never wanted government to control religion, and 2) we then enacted laws to ensure this would not happen, i.e., Congress cannot make laws establishing religion. Thus, in *that sense*, our government was indeed, as the Treaty states, not "per se" founded on the Christian faith. Yet clearly our entire socioeconomic culture was "founded" on Christian principles.

In other words, while we wanted to do away with a government *controlled* by religion, this did not mean that the majority culture was not established on Christian values, as the evidence has shown. And under Brewer's definition, where the majority professed Christianity, all of these factors combined made this nation Christian. The treaty is therefore not contradictory with the position of this book. In addition, the purpose of the treaty was to create peace with a Muslim nation by highlighting the truth that one religion did not *directly* control the State.

Notes

1. David Josiah Brewer, *The United States: A Christian Nation* (Philadelphia, PA: The John C. Winston Company, 1905) 11, 12 (Emphasis added).
2. *Ibid.*, 13.
3. *Ibid.*
4. *Ibid.*, 14.
5. *Ibid.*, 18.
6. *Ibid.*, 22.
7. *Ibid.*, 31-32.
8. *Church of the Holy Trinity v. United States*, 143 U.S. 457 (1892) 470 (Emphasis added).
9. Andrew A. Lipscomb, Editor-in-Chief, *The Writings of Thomas Jefferson,* Vol. 13 (Washington, D.C.: The Thomas Jefferson Memorial Association, 1903) 293.
10. Gary Scott Smith, *Faith and the Presidency: From George Washington to George W. Bush* (New York, NY: Oxford University Press, 2006) 5. *OUP Material: pp.5, 14 & 17 extracts (45 words) from Faith and the Presidency: From George Washington to George W. Bush by Gary Scott Smith (2006). By permission of Oxford University Press, Inc. www.oup.com.*
11. *Ibid.*
12. *Ibid.*, 17.

13. *Ibid.*, 5.
14. *Ibid.*
15. *Ibid.*
16. *Ibid.*, 14.
17. Gary Langer. (2004, July 18). Poll: Most Americans Say They're Christian Varies Greatly From the World at Large. *ABC News*. Retrieved November 3, 2010, from http://abcnews.go.com/sections/us/DailyNews/beliefnet_poll_010718.html.
18. *People v. Ruggles*, 8 Johns. R. 290 (N.Y. 1811) 296-297.
19. Michael Collins & Matthew A. Price, *The Story of Christianity* (New York, NY: DK Publishing, Inc., 1999) 129.
20. *Ibid.*, 155.
21. *Ibid.*, 156-157.
22. *Ibid.*, 157.
23. *Ibid.*, 162.
24. Alan Charles Kors, Editor, *Encyclopedia of the Enlightenment,* Vol. 2 (New York, NY: Oxford University Press, 2003) 73-74.
25. *Ibid.*, 74.
26. *Ibid.*, 75.
27. *Ibid.*
28. Collins, 174-175.
29. *Ibid.*, 155.
30. *Ibid.*, 174.

Study Notes

Study Notes

Chapter 2: Prosperity of a Nation Tied to Trust in God

Although there has been much controversy over whether George Washington, our first president (1789-1797), was a Christian, a Deist or a Freemason, there is no denying that his foundation was Christian. Washington served two consecutive terms as president and was Commander-in-Chief of the Continental Army in the American Revolutionary War.

Let's look at a statement he made to the Delaware Native American chiefs in 1779:

> You...wish to learn our...ways of life, and...above all the Religion of Jesus Christ...these will make you a greater and happier people than you are. Congress will do everything they can to assist you in this wise intention; and to tie the knot of friendship and union so fast, that nothing shall ever be able to lose it.[1]

Washington then wrote in his 1796 Farewell Address:

> Of all the dispositions and habits which *lead to political prosperity, religion and morality are indispensable supports.* In vain would that man claim the tribute of Patriotism, who should labor to subvert these great Pillars of human happiness, these firmest props of the duties of Men and Citizens. The mere politician equally with the pious man ought to respect and to cherish them. A volume could not trace all their connections with private and public felicity. Let it simply be asked where is the security for property, for reputation, for life, if the sense of religious obligation desert the oaths, which are the instruments of investigation in Courts of Justice? And *let us with caution indulge the supposition that morality can be maintained without religion....*Whatever may be conceded to the influence of refined education on minds of peculiar structure, reason and experience both forbid us to expect that national morality can prevail in exclusion of religious principle.[2]

I agree with President Washington's farewell address statement above that political prosperity is tied to religion and morality. I would go further to state that the social and economic prosperity of a nation is also directly tied to its religious prosperity. Washington noted that public happiness is connected to religious prosperity. He concluded that there is no security for anything we own, or even our own lives, if our religious values desert our oaths or our laws! He cautioned *not* to determine that we can maintain morality in society without religion, even where we pride ourselves on being refined by education. Washington clearly here admonished Americans not to lose our values, which are grounded in religion. These Christian principles are the backbone of our laws.

We can look at Washington's position from a practical standpoint, which is that we need the moral principles of religion where they are the basis for our laws. To remove them would mean sure mayhem and disorder in our society.

However, I would also add that, under biblical Christian principles, when a culture finds its roots in Christianity and then turns away from God, that society inevitably will see a decline in its political and socioeconomic prosperity. Satan gains access to that land and comes in to destroy. We lose God's blessings because we no longer trust in Him.

One biblical example of this is the children of Israel in the book of Judges. When they forsook God, He allowed them to fall into the hands of their enemies. When they returned unto God, He restored or revived them. God is a gracious God, slow to anger, and plentiful in mercy. He would later deliver them from various forms of bondage, including Babylonian captivity and Egyptian enslavement.

Corporate Fasting and Repentance as a Foundation

Even from the beginning, in our fight for independence, America trusted in Jesus for sure victory. This republic adhered to the principles of fasting, repentance and prayer as a way to defeat a country which was much more powerful. In order to win that war and later become the most powerful country in the world, we put God first.

The American Revolutionary War occurred between 1775 and 1783. It was a war fought for the independence of the United States from Britain. There were initially thirteen British colonies in North America that fought against Britain, but the war ended with several great powers of Europe involved. Through the help of God, America was able to obtain assistance from France, and then from other countries that supported France.

Let's look at a statement made by one of the founding fathers, Benjamin Franklin (after the

Revolutionary War), at the Convention held to compose the Constitution. He said:

> In the beginning of the contest with Britain, when we were sensible of danger, *we had daily prayers in this room for the divine protection*! Our prayers, sir, were heard; and they were graciously answered. All of us, who were engaged in the struggle, must have observed *frequent instances of a superintending providence in our favor*. To that kind providence we owe this happy opportunity of consulting in peace on the means of establishing our future national felicity. *And have we now forgotten that powerful friend*? Or do we imagine that we no longer need its assistance?
>
> I have lived, sir, a long time; and *the longer I live, the more convincing proofs I see of this truth, that God governs in the affairs of men*! And if a sparrow cannot fall to the ground without his notice, it is probable that an empire can rise without his aid? We have been assured, sir, in the sacred writings, that 'except the lord build the house, they labor in vain that build it.' I firmly believe this; and I also believe that without his concurring aid, we shall succeed in this political building no better than the builders of Babel.[3]

The war ended with America formally declaring its sovereignty in 1776 through the Declaration of Independence, written by Thomas Jefferson.

Daily prayer during the Revolutionary War was, in and of itself, a sure sign of revival and faith in God. Some would contradict by arguing that Benjamin Franklin was a Deist. Although Franklin may have been influenced by Deism at some point in his life, he noted in the quotation above that it was God's protection that enabled us to win victory over our enemies.

I believe Franklin meant the Christian God. Why? Deists do not believe that their god interferes in the affairs of men. He earnestly admonished that we not forget this powerful Friend's intervention. In addition, Franklin mentioned the builders of Babel in the quotation above, which directly referenced the story of Babel in the Christian Bible. He also indirectly referenced Psalm 127, verse 1, which speaks of "the Lord building the house," stating that he firmly believed this. Franklin thereafter noted that the longer he lived, the more convincing proofs he had seen that God governs our affairs.

That speech was made near the end of Franklin's life, and I would contend that he had been given sufficient proof of the Christian God's Divine intervention. Arguably, he may have left any Deist influences behind before he died. Some reference the fact that he may have claimed Deist influence as a youth; but certainly people can change their beliefs over time.

It would grieve the hearts of those who valiantly gave their lives for this great country to see that we have turned our backs on the very One who won us the victory from the beginning. We have taken prayer out of schools, and we are challenging the very motto of the United States: "In God We Trust." Some want to remove the Ten Commandments from the US Supreme Court building. Supernatural intervention won the War of Independence for America, and as Franklin would say, "Have we now forgotten this powerful Friend?"

In the 1800s, Alexis de Tocqueville, a French political thinker, examined many social issues. He commented on the influence of Christianity in America:

> ...In the United States the sovereign authority is religious, and consequently hypocrisy must be common; but *there is no country in the whole world in which the Christian religion retains a greater influence over the souls of men than in America* and there can be no greater proof of its utility, and of its conformity to human nature, than that its influence is

most powerfully felt over the *most enlightened and free nation* of the earth…

Upon my arrival in the United States, the religious aspect of the country was the first thing that struck my attention; and the longer I stayed there, the more did I perceive the *great political consequences resulting from this state of things*, to which I was unaccustomed. In France I had almost always seen the spirit of religion and the spirit of freedom pursuing courses diametrically opposed to each other; but in America I found that they were intimately united, and that they reigned in common over the same country.[4]

Clearly, the historical evidence and record presented thus far overwhelmingly support the argument that many, including the forefathers, believed America prospered because of its Christian roots. "Freedom" was never supposed to do away with this Christian foundation.

Court decisions giving the right to abortion, which Christianity considers as murder (although God forgives those who commit this sin if they come to Him in repentance), must be reversed. Christian prayer must be once again allowed in our public schools. To reverse these decisions would not violate our Constitution, but would adhere to the values and traditions we have held from the beginning.

When we re-implement Christian values into our legal, governmental and business structures, we will see this great country become what it used to be. I discuss the principle of the "Seven Mountains of influence in culture" later in the book; we will look at the value systems of these critical areas, and how these must be changed in order to turn everything around.

We have all sinned and fallen short of the glory of God. The Lord is shaking the Church as well as the entire United States and the world. Will we heed His call and fall to our knees in repentance?

Notes

1. Milo M. Quaife, Editor, *Collections, Volume XXIII* (Madison, WI: State Historical Society of Wisconsin, 1916) 323.
2. Thomas Ankle Clark, B.L., Editor, *Washington's Farewell Address Webster's Bunker Hill Oration* (New York, NY: Charles Scribner's Sons, 1908) 14 (Emphasis added).
3. Walter Isaacson, Editor, *A Benjamin Franklin Reader* (New York, NY, Simon & Schuster Paperbacks, 2003) 362 (Emphasis added). *Reprinted with permission of Simon & Schuster, Inc. from A BENJAMIN FRANKLIN READER edited and annotated by Walter*

Isaacson. Copyright © 2003 by Walter Isaacson.

4. Henry Reeve, Translator, Alexis de Tocqueville, *Democracy in America* (New York, NY: Edward Walker, 1847) 332, 337 (Emphasis added).

Study Notes

Study Notes

Chapter 3: Awakenings, Revivals and America

In this section, I have done my best to summarize some of the religious revival or awakening moves of God over the past centuries of American history. Some may differ as to what period they categorize as an awakening or revival. As you read my understanding of these events, please keep in mind that this is not an all-inclusive outline of revival history, but highlights *some* of the transforming Christian events I believe have impacted the social fiber of America and the world.

I am going to use the term "revival" to mean restoring religious and moral awareness. In Christian culture, a revival refers to a time period of great spiritual rebirth. Some churches may experience their own unique times of revival or rejuvenation of both the saved and unsaved. An "awakening" I will call a large-scale revival that occurs both locally and globally over a certain period of time.

Both individual church revivals and global awakenings involve sincere repentance and transformation. A sure test for true awakening is noting whether a large number of the unsaved come to Christ for the first time. The Spirit of the Lord will not just revitalize the saved population, but will draw the unsaved unto Himself.

Valid awakenings often radically shake and revolutionize civilization's culture. If we look at history, we see that God usually answers the sincere cry of His people for Divine intervention, especially after there has been a deterioration of Christian values in that culture. As was the case with the children of Israel, through revival, God will bring people back to Himself. He uses men and women as conduits to transform the spiritual, socioeconomic and political culture both locally and nationally.

Revival History

I will now identify what I believe to be several approximate time periods of revivals or awakenings in the United States and the world.

First Awakening
1739-1745

As stated previously, the Protestant Reformation which ended in 1648 after intense religious wars, resulted in a decentralization of the Catholic

Church's authority in Europe. Many were unhappy with the intermingling of the Church with government in Europe.[1]

Catholic and Protestant had fought in bloody wars, while political rulers used this opportunity to bring down the Catholic Church's territorial and political control.[2] The first colonists, who were Puritans (English Protestants), fled from Britain in the 1600s, angry at the government's meddling in religious matters. English Protestant reformers had been burned at the stake in Britain. The Puritans were not pleased with the British government's interference in the life of clergy and its attempts to suppress public religious gatherings. They migrated to new lands so that they could be free to practice religion as they chose.[3]

Again, as discussed in Chapter 1, the wars that resulted from the Protestant Reformation led to anti-Christian responses. Philosophers and scientists started to explain human matters and the world at large in a non-religious, secular manner. Yet at the same time, some of the greatest Christian revivals took place. As philosophers emerged, so did revivalists.[4]

Thus, as I noted in Chapter 1, although Enlightenment or Deist philosophical thinking crept in to affect some, the First Great Awakening also took place during this time period (before the

Revolutionary War) and brought many back to the Christian God.

With its roots in the Protestant Reformation, the First Great Awakening was led in Britain by revivalists John Wesley, Charles Wesley and George Whitefield. Jonathan Edwards was an American (New England) revivalist at the forefront of the Awakening in the US. This movement emphasized the individual religious experience. Preaching styles involved much sensationalism.[5]

The Wesleys led a religious club at Oxford University. The members were later called "Methodists" because they lived a holy lifestyle and methodically followed rules. They reached out to orphanages, schools and jails in London.

In 1738, John preached a message at Oxford on being saved by grace through faith, emphasizing a personal experience with God. He and Charles would later take this message to the streets, churches and public venues in London, which marked the beginning of a Methodist revival. John emphasized that salvation involved the individual's personal experience by exercising faith in Christ. George Whitefield was at the forefront of a revival in the Church of Scotland after being invited in 1741 to speak concerning allegations of Deist and humanistic heresies in Scottish churches.[6]

In the US, the First Great Awakening swept through the colonies. A German in Pennsylvania named Theodore Frelinghuysen started ministering on personal transformation versus observing rituals, and revival began. The Dutch Reformed Church was established in 1737 as a result of his teachings.

However, the real impact of the First Awakening took place in Massachusetts, through the preaching of Jonathan Edwards, a Congregationalist.[7] The theme of his messages was salvation by faith alone. He taught a Calvinistic series of sermons in 1734.[8] John Calvin was a French reformer of the Protestant Reformation period who taught on justification by faith.[9]

Edwards' messages bought people to their knees. After one year, nearly all in his town of Northampton had been converted to Christ. By 1742, the Awakening had worked its way through New England.[10] The revival was prevalent among the Congregationalists of New England, the Presbyterians[11] of New Jersey and Pennsylvania, and among both the Presbyterians and Baptists[12] of Virginia.[13]

Britain Resulting Social Reform

In his book, *A History of Christianity,* Kenneth Scott Latourette noted that during the Awakening, the Industrial Revolution started in Great Britain. Those affected by the revival aspired to decrease the wrongs of the past and make Britain a blessed continent.

Robert Raikes, a layman of the Church of England, started a Sunday School program to teach the poor about morality and religion. The Sunday School Society was developed later in London, and extended these schools for the poor throughout Britain. John Howard, a friend of Wesley, began a prison condition reform movement. In addition, wealthy Evangelicals in a London suburb worked on various philanthropic and religious endeavors, including fighting to abolish slavery.[14] The Awakening also resulted in the start of several missionary societies, including the Baptist Missionary Society and the London Missionary Society.[15]

US Resulting Social Reform

We noted previously that the bloody wars from the Protestant Reformation resulted in anti-Christian and pro-philosophical schools of thought, both abroad and in the US.

It is interesting to note that in his book, Latourette concluded that the war for independence in the US negatively impacted Christianity. Political fighting had taken the focus from religion and resulted in moral decline. In addition, the French Revolution, which took place after America gained its independence, resulted in sympathizers of Rationalism and Deism in the US.[16]

The First Awakening tremendously changed the religious, social and political structure of America. For example, because of highly educated leaders in the movement, many Bible colleges were formed. Schools like Rutgers, Dartmouth, Princeton, Brown and Columbia were founded.

In addition, both Enlightenment philosophers and revivalists promoted democracy, and Christians implemented significant social programs in an effort to help others.[17] Foreign missions agencies, such as the American Board of Commissioners for Foreign Mission, were established.[18] The most significant result of the First Awakening was the development of an Evangelical[19] culture, which can be called unique to America.[20]

Second Awakening
1795-1850s

The Second Great Awakening took place in the US during the late 1700s, after the Revolutionary War and onward. I have outlined below *some* of

the different time periods where this revival re-
emerged.

Again, many colonists in the republic wanted the
Church separate from the State. This idea was not
practiced at the time by any country in Europe.
The new settlers saw freedom to practice one's
faith as a right that should not be violated. I note
again that because many colonists were Puritans
who had escaped from persecution, this belief in
separation was strong. Deists supported this
position as well.[21] Many congregations supported
the Revolutionary War. Puritan Congregationalist
clergy would promote the war in their preaching.
Many soldiers were sent into the war from
Lutheran churches. Only Christian groups like the
Mennonites and Quakers (advocates of non-
violence) refused to support the war.

A Presbyterian minister by the name of John
Witherspoon was one of the signers of the
Declaration of Independence.[22] As mentioned
earlier, the First Amendment was later enacted to
forbid Congress from making laws respecting
religion, although this was not prohibited in the
separate states. However, despite the separation of
Church and State, the government was not anti-
Christian, as noted in Chapter 1 where we looked
at Justice Brewer's analysis.

Post-revolution America dealt with issues such as
the challenge of a rising market economy and a

huge increase in the population. Free thinking, intellectualism and other Enlightenment philosophies continued to infiltrate. Revivalists during this period wanted to again save the country from these ideologies that tried to brand Christianity as superstition.[23] This revival's goal was to purify the nation, and revivalists like Charles Finney (discussed below) advocated freedom for all, including the slaves.

The revival started in 1795 through camp meetings in Tennessee and Kentucky, with tens of thousands in attendance. Fiery evangelists like James McGready and Barton Stone were at the forefront of these meetings.[24] At the camp services, Presbyterians, Baptists and Methodists danced, wept, laughed and groaned.[25] The movement then began to spread westward, with emotional conversions and passionate preaching.[26]

In 1810, it continued with efforts from Timothy Dwight in New England, who was the grandson of Jonathan Edwards and president of Yale University.[27] Revival hit churches and colleges alike in New England. Several series of revivals took place at Yale, starting with Dwight in 1802 and continuing for decades thereafter. Ministers in New England such as Dwight, Lyman Beecher, and Edward Dor Griffin prayed and fasted together, preached together, joined for revival tours and encouraged each other.[28]

Another phase of the Awakening started in 1825, with Presbyterian evangelist Charles Finney at its forefront. Finney was an attorney who had left his practice to preach and used a rhetorical style similar to that used in the courtroom.[29] It is estimated that over half a million people were converted due to his ministry.[30] Reverend Finney preached within the Presbyterian and Congregationalist sector. His message emphasized new birth, individual conversion and social reform issues such as abolition of slavery.[31] Finney was one of the greatest revivalists of the Second Awakening.[32]

Social Reform: US and the World

The Second Awakening tremendously reshaped America's social, political and religious sphere, and some consider it the most important awakening thus far in US history. It provided a pathway to social and political change. Social impacts of the revival included abolitionist activism, as noted with Finney above. There was also an enormous effort to transform and Christianize the culture of America, and then spread the reformation across the globe.[33] Both the First and Second Awakenings reached thousands of the un-Churched through intense preaching, and revolutionized US culture.

Yet the Second Awakening had a more extensive geographical reach and impacted a wider variety of denominations. Baptist and Methodist became the two largest Protestant denominations by the 1850s, thus displacing the Presbyterian, Anglican[34] and Congregationalist groups that had been prevalent in the colonial era.[35] The Second Awakening was a major tool in the formation of Protestant Evangelism. The Awakening later advanced outside of the US, spreading Protestantism and missionary work throughout the world.[36]

In the 19th century, many different Christian denominations sprung up because the US was ripe ground for new theologies. Unfortunately, several religions were also established that are considered cults, such as the Mormons, Jehovah's Witness and Christian Science faiths. These religions were usually headed by founders with allegedly new insights and resulted in very different doctrines, much of them spreading around the world.[37]

1857-1860: Businessman Revival

Some historians would say a Third Great Awakening began in North America in 1857. However, I am going to call this a continuation of the Second Great Awakening, as it seemed to indirectly continue the abolitionist impact.

In 1857, before the Civil War, America faced an economic recession. The stock market fell, banks closed and Americans were confronted with extremely difficult times, similar to what we endure today. Some, like President Abraham Lincoln (see his Second Inaugural Address), believed the later American Civil War (1861-1865) resulted from God's judgment because of the ills of slavery.

Immediately preceding the recession, a revival had emerged called the "Businessman Revival." This renewal took place throughout the US, but especially in urban areas.[38] Instead of different revivalists, the focus was on prayer meetings in churches and auditoriums of downtown business districts. Programs consisted of prayer, singing and testimonies. Leaders were mostly laypeople, although some ministers participated.[39]

The most famous and most publicized of these gatherings took place on Fulton Street in downtown NYC, with Jeremiah Lanphier, a missionary layman, at the forefront. In September of 1957, Mr. Lanphier started daily prayer meetings at noon. In the beginning, very few attended, but membership grew when the financial panic began in October. Other factors that contributed to the growth of this revival included immigration and fast-paced urbanization. The revival spread from the north to the south, and later to the British Isles.[40]

Social issues such as slavery were forbidden from discussion at the 1857 meetings. With its impact throughout the US, the Businessman Revival was the closest to *national* American revival of any period in our history.[41] Over the three-year time span of the meetings, Protestant denomination membership increased to more than 474,000.[42]

In his book *Revivalism and Social Reform In Mid-Nineteenth-Century America*, Timothy L. Smith noted that around 1840 (preceding the Businessman Revival), a great concern for social change had developed among Northern Methodists in the US. Abolitionist periodicals had published articles encouraging reform.[43]

In 1857, a Baptist newspaper called the *Watchman and Reflector* started to campaign for awakenings in New England. Articles in the newspaper from January through April of that year reflected measures by churches to stir up revival in areas such as Charleston, MA, Brooklyn, NY, and New York City.[44]

Smith saw a passion for rejuvenation in the urban religious sphere between 1840 and 1857, and thus rejected the notion that revivalism had died out around 1840. He opined that the 1858 meetings were the end result of previous efforts to bring about a national Pentecost.[45]

Continued Social Reform US

In my opinion, although the issue of slavery was not mentioned directly at the Businessman meetings, that revival most certainly impacted the fight to abolish slavery (abolition followed shortly thereafter). I firmly believe that this prayer movement resulted in the conviction of the conscience of America to end slavery.

One of the concrete social changes that occurred after the 1857 revival was the great effort made to evangelize masses of the poor in NYC. In 1857, teams visited the poor and met their spiritual as well as financial needs. The NY Sunday School Union gave churches the responsibility to visit homes and organize mission Sunday Schools in poor areas.[46]

Revivals thereafter began in places such as Brooklyn, Detroit, Hartford and Buffalo, which had followed the NYC plan to evangelize the poor.[47] Presbyterians in Pittsburgh and Cincinnati preached about prayer and fasting as leaders of the Church pursued national awakening. Soon, Congregational, Baptist and Methodist pastors from around the US united for huge evangelistic meetings.[48] Churches in New England also began days of fasting and prayer.[49]

Another great revivalist who stirred social reform during this time was Dwight L. Moody. He had an early experience in the Businessman Revival, and later was used by the Lord to influence foreign missions, Christian education and literature distribution. Moody also started girls' and boys' schools. As a result, college students later became missionaries and evangelized the masses. He addressed millions through an evangelistic campaign assisted by other churches.[50]

It is a well-known fact that the American Civil War from 1861 to 1865 resulted in over half a million deaths. However, a fact not mentioned in history classes is that both the Confederate (Southern) and Union (Northern) armies during the war were touched by revival. Everywhere they encamped, soldiers would hold religious services. Some believe this was a continuation of the 1857 revival. Estimates of conversions are from 150,000 to 200,000 in the Union army and approximately 150,000 in the Confederate army.[51]

In 1862, President Lincoln talked of freeing the slaves through the Emancipation Proclamation. Slavery was abolished in 1865 through the 13th Amendment of the United States Constitution.

I have categorized the other periods below as revivals and not awakenings because they did not have the broader social impact of the First and Second Awakening periods mentioned above and therefore are more accurately noted as revivals.

1906-1909: Azusa Street Revival

A Welsh revival began in 1904 and lasted one year. Although short-lived, this Welsh renewal ignited a later movement in California known as the Azusa Street Revival (approximately 1906-1909). William Seymour, an African American Holiness preacher, was at the forefront of this revival and was greatly influenced by his teacher, Charles Parham, another minister.[52] The Holiness movement promoted a belief in personal sanctification, pursuant to Wesley's teaching.[53] The crowd on Azusa Street was interracial, and everyone was welcomed despite the fact that Jim Crow racial segregation was prevalent. There was an emphasis on the baptism of the Holy Spirit, speaking in tongues, prophesying and healing.[54]

Thus, today's Pentecostal movement was birthed on Azusa Street in Los Angeles, through the leadership of Reverend Seymour.

Other great men and women of God involved in Pentecostal healing movements of the 1900s include John G. Lake, Aimee Simple McPherson, Smith Wigglesworth, and Kathryn Kuhlman. Healing evangelist Billy Graham emerged in the late 1940s, and Benny Hinn from the 1980s to present.

Other movements, such as the Latter Rain movement of the 1950s (doctrine of the last days outpouring on the Church), the Jesus People movement of the 1960s (hippies converted), the Charismatic Movement of the 1960s (traditionally conventional churches influenced by Pentecostalism), the Vineyard Movement in the 1970s (claimed a foundation in Evangelicalism from the past), and the Toronto Outpouring of the 1990s (emphasis on God's love and resulting healing) all can be included in the Pentecostal move of the Holy Spirit.

Of course, there was the Holiness movement of the 1800s, which is at the root of much of Pentecostalism. The Oneness Pentecostal movement of 1914 (broke from Trinitarian view and claimed non-Trinitarian doctrine regarding the Godhead) still follows many Holiness beliefs.

Chapter 8 in this book discusses in detail what our Christian culture is now calling the coming Third Great Awakening.

Religious Revivals Linked to Success of US

I firmly believe that, as was the case with Abraham in the Bible, the American forefathers initially moved out in faith to a land that God showed them and then gave to them. This country was established to be a blessing and an example of freedom from all forms of oppression that had plagued so many other nations.

Because of the past wrongs linked to religion, the forefathers wanted Church and State separate, but the American culture was Christian. When Enlightenment thinking started to infiltrate, the

Lord raised up revivalists to restore the people back to Himself. God blessed this country because of the Christian values embedded in our culture.

But from the very beginning, we see that the enemy fooled some into turning away from their Christian roots. As the nation strayed away, at times because of Enlightenment influences, and at other times because of wrongs such as slavery, the Lord allowed the enemy to bring economic suffering and civil war.

However, as with the children of Israel, when the nation cried out to Him, God again raised up ministers to draw His people back unto Himself. He would then restore peace and rejuvenate the economy (heal the land). It is clear that before and subsequent to America's independence, local and global reformation swayed the course of this great country and the world. Revive us again, oh Lord.

Notes

1. Collins and Price, 154.
2. *Ibid.*, 127.
3. *Ibid.*,143-144.
4. *Ibid.*, 155.
5. Michael McClymond, Editor, *Encyclopedia of Religious Revivals in America*, Vol. One (A-Z) (Westport, CT: Greenwood Press, 2007) 191-195.
6. Collins and Price, 164-166.

7. Puritan churches where congregation governs own affairs.
8. Collins and Price, 167-168.
9. *Ibid.*, 136.
10. *Ibid.*, 167-168.
11. Calvinist Protestants with roots in Scotland.
12. Doctrine of baptism by immersion and not by sprinkling.
13. McClymond, 191.
14. Kenneth Scott Latourette, *A History of Christianity* (New York, NY: Harper & Brothers, 1953) 1031-1032.
15. *Ibid.*, 1032-1033.
16. *Ibid.*, 1035.
17. Collins and Price, 169.
18. McClymond, 196.
19. Need for personal conversion — based in Protestantism.
20. McClymond, 196.
21. Collins and Price, 174.
22. *Ibid.*, 175.
23. McClymond, 385.
24. Collins and Price, 184.
25. McClymond, 387.
26. Collins and Price, 184.
27. *Ibid.,* 185.
28. McClymond, 388.
29. Collins and Price, 185.
30. *Ibid.*, 186.
31. McClymond, 389.
32. *Ibid.*, 388.
33. *Ibid.*, 386.

34. Reformed Protestants with roots in Church of England.
35. *Ibid.*, 384-386.
36. McClymond, 386.
37. *Ibid.*, 186.
38. *Ibid.*, 362.
39. *Ibid.*
40. McClymond, 362.
41. *Ibid.*
42. *Ibid.*
43. Timothy L. Smith, *Revivalism and Social Reform In Mid-Nineteenth-Century America* (Nashville, TN: Abington Press, 1957) 47.
44. *Ibid.*, 48-49.
45. *Ibid.*, 62.
46. *Ibid.*, 65.
47. *Ibid.*, 66.
48. *Ibid.*
49. *Ibid.*, 67.
50. McClymond, 284-287.
51. *Ibid.*, 117-118.
52. *Ibid.*, 37-38.
53. *Ibid.*, 206.
54. *Ibid.*, 37-38.

Study Notes

Study Notes

Chapter 4: Specific Ways We Have Left God Behind

I have discussed previously some of the ways we have strayed from God. I write this chapter not in a judgmental spirit, but look to the word of God for direction. I have shared already that judgment starts with the Body of Christ. God has been judging all of us and cleansing us from sin, both in the Church as well as in the world.

The religious culture and climate in America has changed tremendously since its inception. For example, it was routine for many public schools in the US to open with oral prayer or Bible reading in the 18th, 19th and early 20th centuries.

In the well-known US Supreme Court cases of *Engel v. Vitale* (1962)[1] and *Abington School District v. Schempp* (1963),[2] precedent was established forbidding state-approved prayer in schools. Also, in the famous *Roe v. Wade* decision of 1973,[3] the US Supreme Court gave women the right to abort a fetus during the first two trimesters of pregnancy.

Let's look at how and when everything started to change.

I noted earlier that past US Supreme Court Justice David Brewer set compelling precedent by formally declaring this nation Christian. As recently as 1931, in *United States v. Macintosh*,[4] the court again held that we are a Christian nation.

But in 1947, things started to shift drastically when the US Supreme Court ruled, in the landmark case of *Everson v. Board of Education*,[5] that the Establishment Clause (separation of Church and State) extended to states. The statute previously only applied to the federal government.

Prior to that case, many states had laws favoring Christianity. Although the *Everson* court ruled that the state could pay the transportation costs of Catholic students, the court saw the basis of those payments as *separate from* religion.

We need to be concerned about the *Everson* opinion. Since 1947, courts have used it as precedent to apply the Establishment Clause to state cases.

Many believe that *Everson* marked a turning point in the interpretation and application of disestablishment law in America. Since then, there have been several cases where the courts ruled for the removal of Christian practices from our common law and culture.

The *Everson* case established faulty precedent because the Establishment Clause prohibits the federal government, namely "Congress," from establishing religion and was not intended to affect the individual states.

Since the mid-nineties, humanists (people who advocate for reason and reject the supernatural) have been fighting against Christianity little by little. They have used the Establishment Clause as a basis to remove Christian laws and customs in states.

Christians must be even more vigilant in the battle to redeem our heritage. We must file lawsuits to reverse cases that oppose our Christian customs. There are compelling arguments that separation of Church and State was meant to give citizens the right to practice any religion or no religion at all, but Christianity was supposed to remain at the foundation of our culture and laws.

And even if cases are not reversed, we must fight to keep what we now have.

We must contact and support organizations such as the ACLJ (American Center for Law and Justice), which defends faith in America. The ACLJ has fought effectively for the right of religious freedom, including protecting the rights of unborn babies. This organization successfully defends the religious heritage of America.

For example, the federal appeals court ruled in favor of the ACLJ when it filed an amicus brief contending that an atheist group, the Freedom from Religious Foundation, did not have standing to sue against the president's calling of a National Day of Prayer. The organization also victoriously defended the constitutionality of the Pledge of Allegiance, the National Motto ("In God We Trust") and the phrase "under God," as well as several other areas of America's religious heritage.

We cannot sit back and allow the enemy (Satan's influence on the minds of people) to finish the job he started. Folks, I hate to say it, but *if something is not done actively and progressively*, the humanists win, and the Church loses.

We not only need a religious revival, we need a transformation in every facet of our culture for God. We need more active efforts to retain our Christian heritage. We thank God for the cases that have kept intact areas such as chaplains opening up congressional sessions, but we cannot fall asleep while the enemy remains vigilant.

When I think of what has been happening to the Christian foundation of America, I think of a building under construction. In order for that building to stand, there are pillars that are initially erected to hold the foundation in place. If those pillars are damaged, that building could very well collapse. If the foundational pillars are not repaired as damage starts to occur, the problem can reach a state where the building cannot be fixed at all, but must be torn down.

By standing back idly while humanists and atheists remove Christian tenets from our common law and culture, we are in essence watching the destruction of the very foundation of America. Our "Christian values" is the material that holds us together. The enemy has blinded our eyes into believing that no real damage is occurring. I have seen many externally beautiful buildings still standing, with structural damage threatening to take them down.

This analogy can also be made to the current "professed majority Christian" society in America. If we examine closely, we realize that even those who claim to be Christian do not adhere to God's laws, but profess Christianity in form or tradition only. This is dangerous. We cannot serve two masters; the Bible tells us we will love one and hate the other. In other words, we have allowed intellectualism and humanism to water down the commandments of the Lord.

A true Christian cannot advocate for abortion, knowing that God breathes life into each womb. Again, God gives grace to those who come to Him in repentance after sinning in this way, especially since some really believe that there is no life at conception. This is why it is imperative that we share God's position on this matter. If Christians stand by and do nothing (not preach the true gospel or not challenge the reversal of laws contradicting biblical precepts), then very soon all of the foundational pillars will be pulled out from under us. Without us realizing it, the damage will then be too great for repair.

We must do something now before it is too late. We must fight back now, or else one day we will wake up and realize that the precepts of God have been completely removed from our culture (seemingly overnight), and that too much damage has been done to reverse the changes. Then the entire structure will come tumbling down. Satan will continue to bring financial and other curses, and we will not have God's protection.

This is a serious state of affairs, folks. I write this message passionately. As Christians, we should be well aware of the dangers.

Let's go on to examine some of the Christian tenets that remain and others that have been removed. I just want to reiterate now that, as is the case with our standing on polygamy, many of the principles governing American law came directly from the Christian Bible, which rules adultery, and therefore polygamy, a sin.

We thank God that the Christian sin of polygamy is still forbidden by our laws. The US Supreme Court, in *The Church of Jesus Christ of Latter Day Saints v. United States,*[6] forbade polygamy in 1890, ruling, "It is contrary to the spirit of Christianity and of the civilization which Christianity has produced in the Western world." Again, two years later, in *Holy Trinity* cited earlier in this book, the court discussed the history and prominent role of religion in US laws, business, customs, and society.

I want to now address the issue of homosexuality. I address this issue with caution, because in the Christian faith we love and welcome everyone. I want to emphatically state that what I am about to share is not a message of intolerance.

As Christians, we are simply trying to follow God's laws. I have stated over and over that there is none without sin, and that God is judging the Church as well. He is asking us all to purify our lives. The truth is, we all must repent and daily try to live according to God's precepts.

I want to give some background here because too often the enemy tries to present the argument that Christians are hateful. Think about it: if any of us sincerely believed that a behavior could result in someone being condemned to hell, we would not be able to rest until that person was warned about that behavior.

Therefore, Christians are wrongfully labeled as intolerant. It is because of the love we have for humanity why we reach out. We are simply trying to relay what we believe God says concerning a particular subject. We want to bring the message of salvation from eternal hell to the lost. Folks, we are trying to help. The problem is that we have done it in a judgmental manner. Jesus is love.

Before you write off what I am about to state as hate, please consider all that I write on this topic.

Jesus loves everyone, even those who violate His statutes. The religious leaders in Jesus' time were quick to advocate that the woman caught in adultery be stoned to death, when they themselves were sinners. This is why Jesus said that only the one without sin could cast the first stone. However, He also told the adulterous woman to go and sin no more. I love Jesus. He is full of grace.

John 8 states:

> 1 Jesus went unto the Mount of Olives. 2 And early in the morning he came again into the temple, and all the people came unto him; and he sat down, and taught

them. 3 And the scribes and Pharisees brought unto him a woman taken in adultery; and when they had set her in the midst, 4 They say unto him, Master, this woman was taken in adultery, in the very act. 5 Now Moses in the law commanded us, that such should be stoned: but what sayest thou? 6 This they said, tempting him, that they might have to accuse him. But Jesus stooped down, and with *his* finger wrote on the ground, *as though he heard them not*.7 So when they continued asking him, he lifted up himself, and said unto them, He that is without sin among you, let him first cast a stone at her. 8 And again he stooped down, and wrote on the ground. 9 And they which heard *it*, being convicted by *their own* conscience, went out one by one, beginning at the eldest, *even* unto the last: and Jesus was left alone, and the woman standing in the midst.10 When Jesus had lifted up himself, and saw none but the woman, he said unto her, Woman, where are those thine accusers? hath no man condemned thee? 11 She said, No man, Lord. And Jesus said unto her, Neither do I condemn thee: go, and sin no more (John 8: 1-11).

Although Christians love every human being, the Bible teaches that homosexuality is a sin. The Bible also explains that God's ways are not our ways, and His thoughts are far above our thoughts. How can the creation speak against the laws of the Creator or against the Creator Himself?

The Bible instructs us that God created a man for a woman. He also decrees fornication a sin. God's love for everyone does not erase the fact that He declares certain conduct as sinful. This is the case with homosexuality.

Christians believe that there is a negative spiritual influence behind homosexuality (as with "all" sin), and that an individual can be delivered from this influence. I believe Satan has fooled people into believing that this area does not violate God's laws. Anyone is entitled to disagree. We can even agree to disagree. I have personally heard testimonies of people who have been supernaturally changed in this area and no longer have a desire for same-sex relationships.

I have felt God's heart literally beating with love for those who consider themselves homosexual. Even if you disagree with my biblical beliefs, I have one question to ask. If you feel that you fall within this category, would you be willing to find a Christian church and receive prayer before making a decision that what I say is not true?

One day I had a very interesting discussion with a co-worker. I shared with him that the Bible teaches us about generational curses and influences, and that homosexuality can be passed down as a spiritual influence from generation to generation. He then said excitedly, "This may fit into the argument some have that they were born like this."

We had disagreed amicably on many issues relating to Christianity and this may have been our first possible common ground. He said, "So it can be a spiritual genetic influence?" I countered that although I do not believe homosexuality is "genetic," it is often passed down spiritually through the generations. In a lot of cases, if the parents and grandparents are honest, they themselves will confess to having gone through same-sex experiences, many times from abusive situations in childhood perpetrated by adults against children.

Only the truth will expose Satan's lies. Listen to me, people: the reality is that God destroyed Sodom and Gomorrah by fire in the Bible because of the prevalence of this sin. The New Testament tells us that end-time sins include people who are without "natural affection," which includes homosexuality (2 Tim. 3:3). Romans 1, verses 26-27, speak against lesbian relationships and men desiring men. In 1 Corinthians 6, verses 9-10, the Bible states:

> Do not be deceived: Neither the sexually immoral nor idolaters nor adulterers nor

male prostitutes nor *homosexual offenders* nor thieves nor the greedy nor drunkards nor slanderers nor swindlers will inherit the kingdom of God (NIV, Emphasis added).

Notice that "homosexuality" is included among "slander." Therefore, those who judge homosexuals, yet are gossiping about their neighbors, should take the mote out of their own eyes before trying to deliver their brothers or sisters.

God is faithful to deliver His people from *all strongholds*. If you are homosexual, would you consider giving Jesus a chance to prove this word true?

Although we do not recognize same-sex marriages federally in the US, some states currently approve these unions. In July of 2011, New York became one of those states. As stated previously, the Bible teaches that God will judge a country based on a position that violates His laws.

Let's next look at the issue of war. God is not, per se, against war. There are times when we must defend our nation through war. But if we enter a country for economic reasons alone (such as for oil) to wage war, then God will judge that action. Some argue that we have done this in the past. Again, a country must legitimately defend itself.

But going back to the theme of repentance for areas where we may have missed the mark: if our motives for war were ever based on greed, God would judge those actions.

What is Blinding our Eyes?

Some contend that God is not real because He would not allow poverty and hunger. I have had many discussions with agnostics and atheists concerning their lack of belief. I can discuss this issue peaceably with them because I refuse to get offended by anything said. I listen to people so that I can understand where they are coming from. Many are outraged because they believe our "so-called" God allows destruction as a form of judgment.

I once heard an atheist curse God to my face. I didn't flinch. I then informed her that God loves her. This act humbled the atheist tremendously. She looked at me in amazement and expressed to me that I must really be grounded in my faith to not have responded back in anger when she attacked my God.

I previously witnessed to an atheist group online. I asked the participants in the forum to consider the laws that govern our society. Those laws were enacted to create order. I do not agree with capital punishment, and yet certain states uphold this form of penalty for gross disobedience of the law.

Although I do not agree with that law, I submit myself to the rules created to prevent lawlessness.

I then told the group to consider God as the *ultimate Body of government*, with His own laws in place for humanity.

We may not always agree with the punishment God renders for violation of His statutes, but we must submit ourselves to His authority. Moses interceded time and time again and asked God to not destroy the people because of their sin.

Why should we submit unto God? Because He created the world, and with one breath He can destroy it. It is just that simple, and seems actually quite *logical* to me.

We do not fully understand His ways; it is therefore pointless to use human reasoning to question the One who created us. The Bible advises us that His thoughts are so far above our thoughts.

Most often, the minds of humanists must find logical explanations for everything and reject the supernatural. Because they do not believe God exists, it may be easy to then refute the conclusion that we must submit to His authority. This explains why the Enlightenment thinkers tried to displace Christianity.

I often share with atheists that salvation is a personal experience with God. I elaborate that although I also have a logical mind, God has proven Himself to me on so many occasions. I have seen many healings at the hand of my God, and therefore no one can effectively dispute or take away my personal testimony.

I challenge atheists to pray and ask Jesus to reveal the truth of the gospel. This would seem *logical*. If He is not real, then there can be no harm in this prayer. The Bible tells us that the entire creation has some innate knowledge of God (Rom. 8:19-23).

We must then be willing to accept the truth if God proves He is real. How does He do this? In past dispensations He would appear before man. But in this age, God moves in a variety of ways. For example, if we pray to God for healing and we are then healed, we must not turn away from the truth.

A skeptic new believer who attended one of my services years ago had been afflicted for thirty years with cirrhosis of the liver. I prayed with him and told him God had healed the liver. He was amazed when his next doctor's report showed no sign of the disease! That is compelling proof.

I challenge everyone reading this book to ask Him to reveal Himself. One lady told me that after making that request, she felt a powerful Presence wash over her and she began to cry. Thoughts of suicide then left her mind. That is good proof.

Do not reject Him if He touches your life in some way. Instead, immediately find a Christian church near you and keep pressing in. He will give salvation, peace, joy and hope to everyone who asks.

Other times we can pray specifically for a material need in our lives. I have prayed countless times for people in need of jobs, and God miraculously provided.

I want to note here that our prayers must line up with God's will in order for them to be answered. But I believe He gives a lot of grace to new converts. He is not just going to bless us with a million dollars because we "want it." Why not? Money can be the root of all evil. Many are not responsible enough or grounded enough in faith to handle that kind of wealth. The Lord will not bless us with something that will destroy our lives or take us off course from serving Him.

However, I want to also emphasize that He can bless us with great wealth *at His appointed time*. Over and over in the Bible He allowed the Israelites to walk away with the wealth of their enemies. In this dispensation, the wealth of the unjust will be transferred to the just. This simply means that He will open up avenues for wealth transfer, including promotion for us even when others are laid off.

I will now continue with my past appeal to the online atheist group. I pointed out that if we die, and atheists are correct in reasoning, nothing happens and I have nothing to lose. But if I am right, then there is an eternity of hell awaiting. It would therefore make sense to pray and ask God to reveal Himself.

God represents love and mercy, but when we violate His laws, He will bring judgment. Psalm 18, verses 7-15, describes some attributes of the Lord:

> [7]Then the earth shook and trembled; the foundations also of the hills moved and were shaken, because he was wroth. [8]There went up a smoke out of his nostrils, and fire out of his mouth devoured: coals were kindled by it. [9]He bowed the heavens also, and came down: and darkness was under his feet. [10]And he rode upon a cherub, and did fly: yea, he did fly upon the wings of the wind. [11]He made darkness his secret place; his pavilion round about him were dark waters and thick clouds of the skies. [12]At the brightness that was before him his thick clouds passed, hail stones and coals of fire. [13]The LORD also thundered in the heavens, and the Highest gave his voice;

> hail stones and coals of fire. [14]Yea, he sent
> out his arrows, and scattered them; and he
> shot out lightnings, and discomfited them.
> [15]Then the channels of waters were seen,
> and the foundations of the world were
> discovered at thy rebuke, O LORD, at the
> blast of the breath of thy nostrils.

The Bible always describes lightnings and thunder around the throne of God, as well as fire. The Holy Spirit is often described in the Bible as wind, fire and water. For those who do not believe God would allow catastrophes, I remind them that in the days of Noah, He destroyed nearly the entire human race because of sin.

None of us are guaranteed today or tomorrow; life is indeed quite fleeting. Children who die go home to be with the Lord anyway (absent from the body, but present with the Lord). His ways are not our ways. The Bible describes Him as a God of love and mercy (see prior example of Jesus' mercy toward the woman caught in adultery), but He can and *does* bring judgment.

People have a hard time accepting that. But it is the truth. Again, how can the creation fight against the laws of the Creator? That is the problem: our intellect and reasoning is in the way of truth.

I will note here that I do not believe that the Lord caused the fall of the Twin Towers (World Trade

Center); but I do believe that because we were not praying as we should against the attacks of the enemy (see Chapter 8 where I discuss our 2011 prayers in NYC against terrorism and the success of those prayers), we were not as protected as we could have been.

Psalm 18 also describes one other powerful attribute of the Lord, which is *protector*. Demonic terrorist forces launched an attack against this nation and continue to threaten our country. We must actively seek God's protection through fervent prayer.

There are territorial demonic forces assigned by Satan over cities, regions, and nations. These evil forces are sent to blind the eyes of the people to the truth about Jesus Christ. We can research a city or a nation's history in order to find out what demonic strongholds influence the minds of the people.

I realized in 2010 through a series of dreams, together with my research of New York City and the US, that certain principalities were in place, and that these influences had to be broken in order for us to see revival in New York and America. I have already mentioned strongholds such as worship of money and freedom, as well as the forsaking of Christianity.

From 2008 onward, the Lord instructed me to walk and pray in the Wall Street and downtown areas of Manhattan, including marching around the Ground Zero site and by the East and Hudson Rivers. I asked for God's grace, protection and provision. I knew more darkness would cover the land, but I felt passionate about my call to pray for His Divine intervention. He gave me several revelatory dreams about my commission to the area. I had no idea before 2008 that God had called me to Manhattan. The Lord told me that those revelations were key to revival for the city and country.

Notes

1. *Engel v. Vitale*, 370 U.S. 421 (1962).
2. *Abington School District v. Schempp*, 374 U.S. 203 (1963).
3. *Roe v. Wade*, 410 U.S. 113 (1973).
4. *United States v. Macintosh*, 283 U.S. 605 (1931).
5. *Everson v. Board of Education*, 330 U.S. 1 (1947).
6. *The Church of Jesus Christ of Latter Day Saints v. United States*, 136 U.S. 1 (1890) 49.

Study Notes

Study Notes

Chapter 5: Foundation Shaking

The Lord has been shaking things locally and worldwide, so that we can turn to Him. We are moving from the Church-age to the Kingdom-age, which will be discussed in Chapter 6. The kingdoms of this world must become the Kingdoms of our God. This does not mean that religion will rule the State, just that Christian principles must be restored both in the Church and the world, so that the State can prosper.

Ezekiel 13, verse 14, states, "I will break down the wall you have plastered with untempered mortar, and bring it down to the ground, so that its foundation will be uncovered." The Lord will bring change, not only in terms of delivering people from sin, but in terms of reversing anti-Christian laws in order to lay a new foundation – that is, if we will let Him. Isaiah 58, verse 12, states that the "foundations of many generations" shall be raised up, and God's people will be called the "restorers" of streets to dwell in.

Revival and awakening will sweep through America as Jesus Christ becomes the Chief cornerstone upon which we rebuild our values. We can ultimately win the spiritual war Satan has launched against this nation.

Enemy Attack on Church and World

I have stated from the beginning of this book that I am describing the enemy's attack, not just on the world, but also the Church. We, too, must close the door to sin so that we can prosper.

In a dream I had around 2007, there was a flood that came. I got caught in the flood waters, and the waves were so overwhelming that I could have drowned. In fact, I saw a minister being carried downstream and helplessly waving at me for assistance. But she was too far off, and I had to watch the waves ahead of me which threatened to carry "me" away. I knew that woman didn't make it. I did not know how to swim, but I learned how to ride the waves as they came.

Eventually the water subsided, and I ended up on a large property with a wide stretch of land. It seemed to be located in a wealthy Jewish area. I walked to the door of a large house, and a blonde lady opened the door. In her hand, she carried a huge bed headboard of metal overlaid with gold. She presented me with this gift, but as I reached to grab it she said to wait, that if I picked it up too soon, it would kill me. We both knew what she meant: I was not ready to take hold of it (my true calling in God), and I had suffered some injuries from the flood I had just come out of. I needed time to heal, especially in my mind. In addition, she told me to finish my journey and then come back for the gift.

I looked down the road and saw the stretch I had to walk. It seemed as if I had to travel on a pathway that would lead to a park area, and I knew more floods were to come. She then injected me with a serum, which immediately brought refreshment from the trauma of the flood. However, I felt that the left portion of my head still was not fully healed.

I knew that this dream represented perilous times for the Church Body, both individually and corporately. The waters would test us to see how much we had allowed Him to cleanse us from sin. Those who would allow the Holy Spirit to renew their hearts would be saved. The Lord is looking for a spotless remnant to carry out His will on earth.

I have mentioned how the Lord took me on a journey of inner healing from sins such as bitterness and unforgiveness, from 2008 to 2010. He tested my heart through persecution, and I found that there was so much resentment and anger there when others would come against me. I had to learn to love others with the love of Christ. The flood waters would have overtaken me. But I prayed and sought God in my wilderness and He gave me a new heart.

The point is, we are all sinners, but change in us can only occur when we learn to trust God to do the work. We cannot do it ourselves. We must come to Him in childlike faith, and He will do a new thing.

Before revival can take place outside of the Church, revival has to take place inside of the Church. This is sure to happen as we keep praying one for another.

I began writing this book in 2009. As I neared completion of this work in 2011, I knew that the Holy Spirit was grieved with the state of affairs in the Body. There are so many schisms, and so much territorialism, jealousy and backbiting in the Church. God is not pleased. He will continue to allow Satan access until we totally submit our wills and our hearts unto Him.

Study Notes

Study Notes

Chapter 6: Kingdom Principles

The Kingdom of Heaven is at Hand

Jesus told His disciples in Matthew 10, verse 7, that the Kingdom of Heaven was at hand. He then commissioned them to perform great miracles, which would be proof of the reality of God's Kingdom. Let us examine some of the principles of "kingdoms."

A kingdom is a realm, territory or a sphere ruled by a sovereign, usually a king. The eternal sovereign God governs the Kingdom of Heaven. Jesus Christ reigns and is seated at the right hand of the Father. The Bible says that His Kingdom shall have no end (Luke 1:33). The Lord wishes to use His people to bring in the greatest harvest of souls the world has ever seen, thus establishing His Kingdom on the earth.

Christians are His governmental branch of kings and priests. Revelation 1, verse 6, states that He has made us kings and priests. Romans 8, verse 17, tells us that we are heirs and joint heirs with Jesus Christ. We are children of the King and joint heirs with Jesus Christ. Isn't that wonderful news?

This means that we are seated in heavenly places with Him. We have been given authority to rule and reign upon the earth. We are a royal priesthood and a holy nation — a peculiar people, the Bible says (I Pet. 2:9).

Why does the Lord want us to be priests and kings on earth? So that we can establish His Kingdom government in this world. If we think about the role of kings, they have dominion and authority to establish law and order in their domains or territories. The Lord has given each of us authority in different areas of influence, as we will discuss later in the section on the Seven Mountains of influence. We must find our sphere of influence and take rule so that His Kingdom can be established.

The Lord is putting reformation fire in the heart of His Church. This revival will cross denominational lines and take on many different manifestations through various Church cultures. There will be a gathering of harvest unlike we have ever seen before. And it will all be about His Kingdom. He will establish His Kingdom here on earth. The wealth of the unrighteous will be transferred to the righteous. This Kingdom will be prosperous and will affect every area of culture in modern society. The kingdoms of this world will become the Kingdoms of our Lord. I discuss later the Abrahamic covenant, and why prosperity for the saints must manifest in order to fulfill God's promise to Abraham and to us (Rom. 4:16).

In 2010, I had a dream about a company of people, including myself, who were rescuing many out of the bellies of killer fishes. Jesus told the disciples to come with Him, and He would make them fishers of men (John 21:1-17). The whole earth is in travail because of the coming of the King – the outpouring of the Spirit of the Lord is at hand.

In Matthew 24, verse 14, Jesus prophesied that the "gospel of the Kingdom" would be preached to all the nations of the world before the end would come. No one knows the hour when Christ will rapture His Bride, but He said to look for the signs which are so prevalent today – wars, rumors of wars, and earthquakes in diverse places. Before the rapture and the tribulation, there must be a massive harvest through a message that "preaches" the Kingdom of heaven and brings in end-time prosperity, in order to fulfill the Abrahamic covenant.

Seven Mountains and Prosperity

Every valley shall be exalted, and every mountain and hill shall be made low: and the crooked shall be made straight, and the rough places plain (Is. 40:4).

There is a teaching today relating to the Seven Mountains of culture. In order to impact the world for Jesus Christ, we must reclaim the Seven Mountains of influence in culture, which are *business, education, arts and entertainment, media, government, family, and religion.* The Church must realize that when we lose our influence, we lose our culture. For too long, these mountains have been valleys for us. Isaiah 40, verse 4, tells us that God will bring down every mountain of the world, and the valleys that the Church has faced will now be exalted. In other words, there will be an exchange.

As I've stated several times, the kingdoms of this world must become the Kingdoms of our God. One of the most important mountains is business. Those who control this mountain control the other mountains, or what influences our culture. This is why prosperity is such a vital part of our message.

We cannot preach on suffering and leave out prosperity. Without sufficient funds, the Church of God is crippled and limited. In Deuteronomy 8, verse 18, the Bible tells us that it is God who gives us power to obtain wealth to establish His covenant with our forefathers, including the promise to Abraham that His seed would inherit the earth. Although greed can and often does pervert the teaching on prosperity, we cannot leave the spiritual law of sowing and reaping out of our message. The Lord will deal with those who allow greed to enter in.

I recently heard a former Jewish Rabbi, who is now a Christian pastor, state that religious Jews believe in and expect their God to prosper them. It is only in the Church where we limit God. The problem has also been wealth in the hands of only the pastors of mega-churches. As God establishes His Kingdom, Christian clergy and lay people alike will prosper.

God is raising up millionaires to fulfill His covenant with Abraham – God's seed will inherit the earth. We will not only have a spiritual awakening, but an economic revival where the Church will take charge of the business mountain and raise up a generation of wealthy Kingdom stewards. The wealth of the unjust must be transferred to the just, and the world will envy God's people. The world will want the "anointing to prosper" that the Church possesses during these dark times.

Prosperity is America's Portion

Abrahamic Covenant

As with Abraham, the Lord told the founding fathers of America to leave their European countries and come to a land that He would show them — a land which has indeed flowed with milk and honey. This act of obedience on the part of Abraham brought about a covenant of blessings or prosperity. The Bible tells us that the benefits of the Abrahamic covenant are ours because we have been adopted into the Kingdom as children of God and joint heirs with Jesus Christ.

The promise the Lord gave unto Abraham, which also applies to the Church, and to America, is as follows:

> And I will make of thee a great nation, and I will bless thee, and make thy name great; and thou shalt be a blessing (Genesis 12:2).

Clearly, Jesus established His covenant promise to America and blessed us. But because of a falling away and a violation of His statutes, judgment has hit the land.

We will look in Chapter 7 at the process of repentance, fasting and prayer as a means to avert God's further judgment and bring blessings. God wants a true Christian nation under God, and then He will restore what the enemy has stolen. Once we turn back to Him, He will bless us. The end-time Church will be a wealthy Church. We will be light in the middle of a dark recession and lead by example.

Joel 2, Isaiah 40, and Isaiah 60 all speak of the darkness that will cover the earth in this time. But

Isaiah 60 tells us that despite the darkness, God's light will shine upon us. Gone are the days of only solo millionaire preachers; God is putting wealth into the hands of everyone. We will take control of the mountain of business and bring wealth into the Kingdom. The systems of poverty, unemployment and lack will be converted to systems of wealth unto God.

Joseph

Joseph was one called by God from before He was born. His brothers were jealous and hated him because God had called him to rule over them. There is a spiritual battle going on to bring America down because we have such deep Christian foundations, with roots in Judaism. God's promise to Joseph and to us is that, as we are obedient to Him, He will give us the best of the land and cause us to prosper in the midst of famine or recession (Gen 37, 39, 41).

Reclaiming the Seven Mountains in American culture is the key to "reformation." The influence at the top of each mountain possesses the power to influence nations. Jesus must be placed as the foundation of each mountain. We must return to "one nation under God."

We have looked at the fact that American democracy is intricately tied to a system of values that is firmly based in the Bible. The plan of the enemy is to rob us of these principles that shaped our existence from the beginning. America represents everything most countries lack — freedom to live our lives without government oppression. But we have gotten so caught up with the term "freedom," that we have come to honor liberty above God. This has resulted in the removal of some Christian tenets from our culture.

Because we have not honored the God who prospered us from the beginning, we have lost the blessings we so desperately need from One who is able to restore our economy and keep us from all evil. The honor of freedom *above* God was never the intent of the forefathers.

I am not advocating that there be no separation of Church and State. I am simply contending that we should reinstitute into our culture previous customs such as prayer in schools, so that we can honor God. Parents could then choose whether or not to allow their children to attend brief prayer sessions before school. I have never heard of a situation where Christian teachings or programs have negatively affected children.

An agnostic friend of mine once said to me that although she did not know if God exists, she was amazed at the sheer anger that people would display at the thought of their children being exposed to Christianity. She then commented that these same parents would pay so much money to take their children to concerts where teen idols promote promiscuity at an early age!

Instead of removing prayer altogether, the courts could have ruled that prayer sessions be administered separately from the general student classes; this would have been a viable alternative.

In addition, we must reverse decisions upholding issues such as the right to abortion. I especially sympathize with women who have been victims of rape and consider abortion; however, that *fact* does not erase the *fact* that these unborn children will never be given chances to live. There are other viable alternatives, such as adoption.

If we want to prosper economically, socially and politically, we must turn back to God.

Study Notes

Study Notes

Chapter 7: The Model: Back to Corporate Fasting and Praying

As we saw earlier, the very beginning of American culture was grounded in prayer and fasting, even while the Revolutionary War ensued. We must go back to those roots. This is why our "returning" is called "revival." We are going back to something we had before, only this time there will be a greater measure of the outpouring of God's Spirit.

I know that there are many prayer formats, but the Lord revealed to me that during this time of national crisis, we must examine similar situations in the Bible and follow the blueprint in order to see breakthrough. We must specifically repent for our sins and the sins of our forefathers, beginning with the Deist and Enlightenment thinking which initially seeped in and corrupted some.

I believe it is of great significance that the first president may have been influenced by these popular philosophies of the intellect or reason. That opening allowed the enemy access to create territorial strongholds over America. These strongholds must be broken through prayer. Pride, greed, and lack of faith in Jesus are all strongholds we must repent from corporately. We must also repent for the sins of 1) worship of freedom above God, and 2) pagan practices such as Freemasonry. Other demonic strongholds include atheism, agnosticism, New Age and the occult, and murder (from abortion to any unjustified killings, including wartime).

In the Church, we must come against spirits of pride, competition, greed, selfish ambition and the like. It is going to take corporate prayer to win the spiritual war for America. It is going to take corporate prayer to defeat terrorism and other evils seeking to take this great nation down.

Joel's Army

In the book of Joel, we see that the prophet spoke about a dark time where there is a turning away from God, the resulting judgment, and ultimately, the fact that the Lord can "repent" (change His mind) from the evil and bring a blessing instead of a curse. As I shared in the beginning of the book, we serve a merciful God who will restore His people if we repent.

Judgment

Joel 2 contains a prophecy about future desolation. Some theologians believe that the army mentioned here is actually an army of revolutionaries who will preach passionately and warn of God's judgment upon the earth because of the ills of the time. I agree with this interpretation. God is raising up some fire-preachers – people such as myself who have been trained in a wilderness period and are passionate to "prepare the way for the coming of the Lord." These are modern day John the Baptists and Elijah types, which I discuss in more detail later.

Joel 2, verse 2, mentions a "day of darkness." Folks, as of the date of the writing of this book, in case you have not noticed, we are in a day of darkness. For example, economic crises have occurred locally and globally, the US recently lost its national credit rating, and one natural disaster after another has hit our land. This is the darkness I saw on the horizon in a dream I had several years ago, which I mention below.

In 2008, before the stock market crashed, I had a dream which I now know predicted that crash. I recall e-mailing the dream to several Church leaders, in desperate hopes of an accurate interpretation. I knew the dream signified impending darkness on America and NYC, but never could I have imagined the economic crash that would shortly occur.

In the dream, I was in a large conference room with other people. There was a huge bay window in the room overlooking a river, with ships passing on the water. While in the room, I looked out of the window and saw darkness in the atmosphere. To the right were one each of two larger-than-life Mickey and Minnie Mouse dolls.

As we passed through the Mickey and Minnie dolls, the atmosphere was very intimidating, but we managed to pass through. As I was seeing all of these things, I recall that there was a short gentleman to the left, and another person to my right whose face I could not remember. I tried to warn them both of the atmosphere and what I was seeing, but they could not see. Then in the distance, I saw what appeared to be a storm brewing—a tornado, to be exact. We were heading right toward the tornado. A voice then said to me, "Speak to it," after which I woke up.

A few weeks after the dream, I was hired for a legal assignment in the Wall Street area of Manhattan. I was not familiar with Wall Street and had never worked there before. I knew the address of the firm was "1 World Financial Center." When I got off the train on the first day, I recall asking people if they were familiar with the address. I was continuously told that it was right across from "Ground Zero." At the time (believe it or not), I had no idea "Ground Zero" was the term for the demolished World Trade Center site.

I later realized that in order to get to my building, I had to circle about two-thirds of the entire expanse of that site. I would then walk around that area over the next eight months, praying for New York City and America as I did. Little did I know that the location of the firm was not only right across from the old World Trade Center location, but was home to many of the companies which later went out of business, partially resulting in the stock market crash that came.

The firm placed those assigned to this project in a large conference room overlooking the Hudson river. We could see the Statue of Liberty from the room. One day, as a few of us stood looking out of the big bay windows, we commented in amazement on how fortunate we were to get a room with such a breathtaking view. I then saw ships passing on the waters of the river. When I looked to my left there was a short man (similar to the man in my dream) staring out of the window also, and all of a sudden the entire dream came back to me.

Directly to the left of the river, I saw the exact location of the World Trade Center site under construction.

I emphasize here that I believe the enemy (not God) caused the World Trade Center attacks, but was able to penetrate only because we were not praying as we could have been. In this dream, I now believe God was simply warning of the recession which was to come (I explain why below), and possibly warning me to pray against another potential terrorist attack.

Several months later, we would hear that we were in the middle of a huge stock market crash. I then heard a prophet refer to the financial crisis as being in the "eye of the storm." I immediately recalled the voice in the dream telling me to "speak to it," and realized that the Lord had assigned me to cover NYC in prayer for God's mercy, blessing and protection.

Thus, the economic recession that followed proved to be the darkness I had dreamed about. And there is more darkness to come, if we do not heed the warning signs. Isaiah 60 speaks of this day of gloom, but notes that the "light of the Lord" shall shine in that day. These are the times we are now living in.

In early 2010, while still in the wilderness, I had yet another dream where I was with a group of young people. We were being used by the Lord to perform powerful miracles. But we seemed to be in training and had to run five miles.

Joel's army will consist of many young people. They will have fire in their spirit, and they will walk in great signs and wonders. Joel 2, verse 3 states that before them is the "garden of Eden," and behind them is the wilderness. This is because they have been trained in the wilderness and are pressing toward restoration of the Kingdom – the "garden of Eden." The garden of Eden also symbolizes all of the blessings that God has for His people.

This army that God is raising up will see the signs of the time – they will be able to see the impending doom and warn the people. These will be warriors – not military warriors, but warriors in the spirit. They will be people who know how to pray (Joel 2:7). These warriors will not just be leaders, but normal, everyday believers with a passion to spread the Good News. They shall run to and fro in the city bringing the Good News. The "climbing through windows" symbolizes the gospel being heard from the streets and through media (Joel 2:9).

Grace: Call to Repentance, Prayer and Fasting

In the early part of Chapter 2 in the book of Joel, there is a warning of impending destruction. In verse 12, we see a call from the Lord to repent so that He can change that judgment and bring a blessing. Verse 12 calls for fasting, weeping, praying, and repenting. The Lord wants us to come to Him with all of our hearts, and not just an outward show.

Verse 13 tells us that we serve a God of grace. This is very important. Most people focus on the judgment, but while I was in the wilderness, the Lord showed me that He is a God of great mercy. He wants so desperately to save His people from the doom to come. Verse 15 admonishes us to "blow the trumpet," or warn of what is to come. We must call a fast, gather the people (even the children) to corporately fast, and appeal to God for grace.

Type of Prayer

We must pay close attention to "how" the Lord instructs us to pray here. Verse 17 of Chapter 2 in Joel says that leaders should cry, "*spare thy people, O Lord, and give not thine heritage to reproach, that the heathen should rule over them: wherefore should they say among the people, where is their God?*" (*Emphasis added*) This is a prototype prayer not just for leaders, but for everyone to pray during these times.

Deliverance and Restoration

Then we see the great delivering hand of the Lord in verse 18 of Chapter 2 in the book of Joel. After the corporate fasting and praying, it says, "then will the Lord be jealous for his land and pity his people." The land of the United States of America belongs to the Lord Jesus Christ. There is a covenant with God that we have broken with sins such as paganism, removing prayer from schools, abortion, and economic greed. We must turn back to Him with all of our hearts. Verse 19 states that then the Lord will bless with corn and wine, which signifies prosperity or a restoration of the economy.

If we want to see America prosperous again, we must follow these principles.

In verse 20, God then promises to remove the northern army with "his face toward the east sea." I believe this represents the armies of terrorism coming against this country from the Middle East. He says He will send our enemies into a barren land. In verse 21, He tells us to "fear not." America is ridden with fear right now. Newspaper reports at the start of the recession in 2008 indicated that people fainted as the stock market crashed.

Economists now label the economic downturn (from 2008 to the present, 2012) as the Great Financial Crisis (GFC), and claim that this is the worst financial plight since the Great Depression (1930s). Stock markets around the world have collapsed. Large financial institutions have folded. The US government bailed out many banks.

No one knows when this global crisis will end. We have seen some brief upturns, but we are still in the eye of the storm.

God promises to restore what the enemy has stolen, and to pour out His Spirit upon all flesh. This will be the greatest outpouring of the Holy Spirit and ingathering of souls in the history of the Church. Why? Because it is the end-time harvest before the rapture of the Church. Jesus said that this "Kingdom gospel" must be preached to the entire world before the end comes (Matt. 24:14).

God's Spiritual, Social and Economic Plan

Joel 2 and Deuteronomy 28 in the Bible give us the blueprint of God's spiritual, social, and economic plan for the nation. We looked previously in depth at Joel 2. In summary, the prophecy in Joel 2 has four parts:

A. **Darkness or famine hits a land** (Joel 2:2)

B. **Spiritual and Cultural Awakening**: The Lord gives instructions on how to pray ("spare people oh God": Joel 2: 17). Revival prayers will lead to a spiritual awakening hitting the land. People will repent and fall to their knees in true worship. Repentance prayer groups will form nationally to cry out to God. This will result in a revolution in the Seven Mountains of our culture as people see the need to restore Christian values back into business, government, media, etc.

Then God will show mercy on the land (Joel 2:18)

C. **Blessings and Protection will result**:
Joel 2:19 The Lord will send wine and oil **(US economy restored)**

Joel 2:20 The Lord will remove the northern army **(protection from terrorist attacks)**

Joel 2: 22-23 Famine over **(including drought from heat)**. The Lord even tells the beast of the field to be not afraid — the Lord will bring the latter rain.

Joel 2:24-25 Floors full of wheat and lost years restored **(Economic Prosperity: jobs, businesses prosper)**

D. **Further Spiritual Awakening:**
Joel 2:28 The Lord will pour His Spirit out on all flesh, and the face of Christianity as we know it will be changed. Miracles, signs and wonders will become the norm in the Church.

***Please see the "prayer model" chart in this chapter, which further describes the Lord's spiritual, social and economic plan (**Deut. 28**), including the Lord establishing us as a holy*

people unto Himself **(reformation of the Seven Mountains of culture: Deut. 28: 9)** *and the reduction of national debt* **(Deut. 28: 12)** *if we obey the Lord's commandments, and the curses that can result if we do not.*

Folks, the promise of deliverance in Joel is for us. Will you give Christ your heart today so that you can be on the road to enlist in His spiritual army and bring about a national revolution?

Jonah

There are many other instances of national crises in the Bible where similar prayers such as the one taught in Joel were used to change God's mind from rendering impending judgment.

In the book of Jonah, we see that God actually sent his prophet Jonah to proclaim total destruction of the great city of Ninevah in forty days (Jonah 3:4). The city was exceedingly evil, and Jonah was happy to preach doom. The turn of events in Jonah shows us the nature of man versus the nature of God. While Jonah thought the people deserved destruction, God had pity on them when they called a fast and cried out to Him for mercy.

When the king of Ninevah heard of the impending destruction, he called a corporate fast and said "Who can tell if God will turn and repent, and turn from his fierce anger, that we perish not?" (Jonah

3:9) Jonah was angry that God showed mercy when the people deserved judgment. But the Lord rebuked Jonah and told him that the great city was spared because there were so many there who did not know the truth (Jonah 4:11).

We must sound the alarm and inform the inhabitants of our cities in America of the impending doom if we do not repent. God is sure to reverse the curse if we are obedient.

Solomon (Davidic Covenant)

In 2 Chronicles, verse 7, we see Solomon dedicating the temple to God, giving us an example of how we should pray. Solomon reminded God of His covenant with David, Solomon's father, that if God's people ever turned away from Him, as long as they humbled themselves in prayer, repented, and turned from their wicked ways, God would forgive and heal their land (2 Chron. 7:14).

Solomon understood covenant relationship with God. The forefathers of America and the majority population established a covenant with God and made this land "one nation under God."

As Christians, we are adopted into the lineage of David, and thus have the full privileges of that Davidic covenant. We must remind God of His word. He said to put Him in remembrance of His word, and that He put His word above His name (Ps. 138:2).

Moses

Moses was an amazing leader. There were many times when God wanted to render harsh judgment upon the Israelites because of disobedience, and he would intercede and cry out for God's mercy. Moses was a selfless leader. His cries to the Lord for mercy held back the hand of judgment on several occasions, and thus we will examine his prayers.

In Exedus 32, the Lord was angry with His people because they had turned to other religions such as witchcraft, and had given credit to other gods for delivering them out of Egypt. They had made graven images. The Lord told Moses to allow Him to destroy the people and bless only Moses, because they were a "stiff-necked" or stubborn people (Exed. 32:8-9). Moses then reminded Him that He had brought the people out of Egypt, and that the enemy would mock them if God forsook them. The Lord then turned from His wrath.

In Deuteronomy 9 verse 28, again Moses interceded and reminded God that the enemy would say that God was not able to bring His people into the land He had promised them, if He destroyed them.

Below are the prayer models we must use in times of national crisis.

Prayer Model

Scripture	Crisis	Corporate or Individual fast/prayer	Result
Joel 2:17	Impending judgment because of sin	**Corporate:** People prayed: *spare thy people, O Lord, and give not thine heritage to reproach, that the heathen should rule over them: wherefore should they say among the people, where is their God?*	God repented (changed His mind) of evil and brought revival, including prosperity
Jonah	Impending judgment because of sin	**Corporate:** People fasted and repented	God repented and did not destroy
2 Chron. 6:24-42; 2 Chron. 7:14 (Davidic Covenant)	Defeated before an enemy because of sin: famine, pestilence, and blight resulted	**Corporate:** If people returned to God, confessed His name, prayed, and made supplication before Him — *humble self, pray and turn from wickedness*	God would hear from heaven and forgive the sins of His people, and bring them back to the land that He had given to them and to their fathers
Deut 9:28	God's impending judgment because of a turning away to witchcraft	**Individual:** Moses Prayed: Let not the enemy triumph and say you were not able to bring your people into the land you promised	God repented from judgment

Ezra 9 and 10	God's impending judgment because people disobeyed: One leader, Ezra, interceded *mainly* for other leaders who had gone astray	**Individual and Corporate:** Ezra wept, fasted and prayed and then the people gathered together and corporately confessed and repented before God, especially the clergy	Revival took place
Daniel 9:4-19	People had been given over to Babylonian captivity because of sin	**Individual:** Daniel confessed sins of people and reminded God that He is a merciful and forgiving God, and that the Lord had brought them out of Egypt with a mighty hand, which made Him reknown (vs. 15)	God revealed to Daniel through His angel, Gabriel, that the people would be restored
		Dan. 9:17 *Hear us for your name's sake* Dan. 9:19 *Hear us because of the city and people called by Your name*	

Deut. 28	Blessings of Obedience	***God's Spiritual, Social and Economic Plan for US*** If we obey God's commandments and instructions	1. Enemies shall flee (**terrorist attacks aborted v.7**) 2. Storehouses will be blessed (**jobs and businesses restored v. 8**) 3. Lord will bring us closer to Himself (**Christian values restored in land v. 9**) 4. All people of earth will see God's blessings and protection and be afraid (**v. 10**) 5. Lord will make goods, land and cattle plenteous (**restore economy v. 11**) 6. We will lend to nations and not borrow (**restore US credit rating/debt reduction v. 12**)

Deut. 28:15-68	Consequences (curses) of disobedience	*God's Judgment because of disobedience*	No rain on land; enemies shall prevail; another nation shall profit from the fruit of the land; land shall become an astonishment unto other nations; other nations shall lend to and be head over that country; people shall be scattered among the nations

Prayer Points US and NYC (Sins we must corporately and individually repent from as a nation)

Anti-Christ Spirit
Deism, Freemasonry and other false religions *(First president and other forefathers may have been influenced by these)*
Idol of freedom above the laws of God
Idolatry
Harlotry
Greed/love of money
Intellectualism above God
Pride
Divorce
Love of power
Atheism
Agnosticism
Abortion
Murder
Homosexuality
Adultery
Pornography
Sexual Sins *(fornication, pornography, prostitution)*
Drug and Alcohol Addictions
All Crime

Pray for God's blessings and protection over America in the following areas:

US debt reduction
NY stock market
Economy
Healthcare
Joblessness/poverty
Homelessness
Terrorism
Protection from natural and man-made catastrophes

Elijah

In this end-time, the Lord is raising up forerunners with the mantles of John the Baptist and Elijah, to "prepare the way of the Lord." These are the people whom He calls to "blow the trumpet," or sound an alarm about the impending judgment spoken of in the book of Joel. When I was first saved, I received a prophesy that I did not understand at the time. The word was that I would be a forerunner and one who would "prepare the way of the Lord."

Years ago, I taught on the radio and entitled the program, "Prepare Ye the Way." I would preach from Isaiah 40, where the Lord said He would make a way in the wilderness, and commissioned the forerunners to sound an alarm. John the Baptist preached repentance because the Kingdom of Heaven was at hand. He was a forerunner who ministered before Jesus' public ministry.

We are now called to prepare the way before the rapture of the Church and the coming of Christ. The Lord has been preparing a people in the wilderness who will sound a warning.

The spirit of Elijah represents turning the hearts of the children back unto the Father, God Himself (Malachi 4:5-6). In addition, we will see earthly fathers and families restored in this time. Also, spiritual fathers commissioned to raise up the next generation, will take their place. Most importantly, God will bring forth these Elijah mantles to turn the wayward hearts of His American children back unto Himself.

Study Notes

Study Notes

Chapter 8: Third Great Awakening

Global Awakening

The Kingdom of heaven is at hand (Matt. 10:7). We are on the verge of a Third Great Awakening, which will be the greatest awakening of all times in Church history. This revival will be unprecedented, and there will never again be any like it (Joel 2:2). The Lord will establish His Kingdom here on earth, and the gates of hell shall not prevail against it.

Although the Bible does not speak of the entire world becoming Christian, there is an awakening coming that will affect and take whole countries and nations for Jesus. America was built on the principles of separation of Church and State, but I believe there is a reformation coming that will tremendously impact the Seven Mountains of influence in this great country. Christians will gain more influence; revival messages will bring our value system more akin to what it started out as – one intricately intertwined with the Jesus of

Christianity. Try as we might, there is no denying that heritage.

The US and the world, as of 2011/2012, are in a great recession, or GFC. The time is ripe once again to bring people back to God.

I have discussed on several occasions in this book the specific ways in which we have moved away from our Christian roots and values. As a result, judgment has hit our land. In August of 2011, the US dropped in its national credit rating for the first time in history. Our problems include the mounting national debt, health care issues, and unemployment.

In August of 2011, New York City felt the tremors of an earthquake for the first time in a century. In that same week, we experienced an unprecedented hurricane threat (Hurricane Irene) which forced the public transportation system to close for the first time due to a natural disaster. Over 250,000 people were evacuated from their homes. Mayor Bloomberg announced the first mandatory evacuation of waterfront areas in NYC.

When I look at all of these "firsts," I realize that God is trying to get our attention. Fortunately, the storm had minimal impact on the state of New York.

Awaken NYC: God Protected from Irene and 9/11 Attack

Before the threat of Hurricane Irene, the Lord had led me to begin a series of open-air meetings in the downtown Manhattan/financial district area of NYC. I was led to name these meetings "Awaken NYC." We started on July 14, 2011, in Foley Square park, and took a break in October of 2011. We plan on resuming the meetings in 2012. We have been corporately fasting and praying under the instructions in the book of Joel.

God has called us to repent and turn back to Him. As a result, we will receive His blessings and protection. Thus, the message I brought to the population there was one of the need for repentance, and a warning that if we did not obey, further judgment could hit our land.

My initial team was very small. A pastor from New Jersey walked by one afternoon, and after listening to me "reason" with the people about America's Christian roots, he came up and told me that I reminded him of the apostle Paul as he presented the gospel before magistrates. He told me that the message I taught needed to be heard nationally.

But I knew it was not God's timing. My specific assignment in 2011 was to bring the message locally for the time being, and to intercede so that the people could see God's power when we submit and pray. If there were no volunteers available, many times I would set up and conduct the meetings alone. I carried the equipment in two suitcases, and one past volunteer jokingly called them the "church on wheels."

I asked the people to corporately repent with me before God and pray for His mercy over NYC. We signed people up to fast with us, and I recall openly on the microphone binding the principalities of greed, pride, and atheism over NYC. I remember wrestling in prayer against specific demonic world rulers assigned to NYC, such as death, financial destruction and terrorism.

I firmly believe that God answered our prayers where Hurricane Irene had minimal impact. I also believe that, because of our petitioning heaven, God protected us from a "real" terrorist threat on 9/11/2011 – a threat which had been advertised in the news. People signed our guestbook to join us in the fast, and I noticed something as we were praying: people were in their cars and passing by, but I could see that they were agreeing with us in prayer!

Some said the storm didn't do much damage in NYC because it was never supposed to be serious anyway. But I beg to differ. The mayor would not have evacuated the city had there not been a "real" threat. I believe that because we were obedient and prayed corporately, God heard our cries for mercy in NYC. He therefore *changed His mind* about the destruction that could have occurred.

We thank God for the billions of dollars and the countless lives He spared because of the corporate repentance of the people of NYC in Foley Square, and because of other Church prayers.

I know that there may be more dark times ahead. But as in the story of the city of Ninevah in the Bible, more people need to hear the message and be given an opportunity to truly repent and come to God. Therefore, I believe disasters such as Hurricane Irene and 9/11/2011 potential terrorist attacks passed us because of the grace of God. But again, we must come back to Him as we hear the message. If we continue to corporately pray and repent, we will continue to see God's mercy.

Occupy Wall Street

On September 17, 2011, after we had been fasting and praying for about two months, a group emerged called "Occupy Wall Street," with complaints about the corruption on Wall Street and in the US government. It is interesting that the group apparently started to mobilize by e-mail on July 16, 2011, two days after we started our open-air prayer meetings in the Wall Street area. Many in that movement are unemployed and/or college students who are afraid of what the future holds.

With high debt and no job prospects, this group has been actively protesting for change.

Although I sympathize with the real concerns of Occupy Wall Street, I believe that breaking the law as we protest, or *angrily* pointing the finger, is not the answer. We are all sinners. There is none righteous. Although we need real solutions (as many in the movement are proposing), I believe that the root problem is America's falling away from God.

Even if we stop the government spending and implement the best economic plan, without God, it will ultimately fail. The Bible tells us that all power belongs to God. With things such as removing prayer from schools and advocating for abortion, many in our culture have missed the mark. Why? Those actions will bring God's judgment, resulting in a famine or economic crisis in the land.

The Bible has many examples of how the Israelites transgressed from God's laws, and the resulting suffering that occurred. Instead of *angrily* pointing the finger, we all need to fall on our knees and pray for God's mercy. Only prayer (coupled, of course, with real solutions as God leads) will turn this economy around. See Chapter 7 for biblical proof that only "God's economic plan" will work.

2011 Church-Ban

Word came to our ministry in November of 2011 that the Second Circuit in New York had ruled that the Board of Education of the City of New York (BOE) could ban churches from meeting in public schools after hours to hold religious worship services, although other non-religious groups could meet without similar restrictions. The case apparently had been ongoing between a church called the Bronx Household of Faith and the BOE for approximately 17 years. The new ruling was issued against the church in June of 2011, the month before we started our Awaken NYC intercession.

In *The Bronx Household of Faith v. Board of Education of the City of New York*, the court acknowledged the right of religious groups to meet and sing, pray or study the Bible (protected speech), but upheld the BOE's ban on "worship services," holding that such *services* (unprotected activity), in effect, turned the school into a church.[1]

Thus, the prohibition was allegedly against the *service*, not the worship itself. So technically a boy scout group could rent the school for Bible study and singing, but when a "church with ordained clergy" met, that activity was held to "consecrate" the school and turn it into a church.[2]

This ruling shocked many in the Church Body (and many outside of the Church).

Ironically, after publicly warning for months in our "Awaken NYC" services that New York needed to come back to God, and that America had gone astray with actions such as taking prayer out of public schools, I then found myself right in the middle of a similar legal church/state dispute.

I learned about this case after nearing completion of the writing of this book. It is a prime example of the falling away I have been describing. This issue directly affects our ministry which, at the time of the negative ruling, *had just started* to utilize one of these public school spaces.

I knew that God had called us to intercede. I also knew that this case was the enemy's attempt to violate the free speech rights of the Church. I was prepared to file my own lawsuit, and then I learned that the Alliance Defense Fund, which represented the church in the first action, had filed a new case. In February of 2012, there seemed to be a shift in the Church's favor. An injunction was issued allowing all churches to continue to worship until the new lawsuit is decided.

I believe God will use this issue to bring the Church together in unity to fight a common foe. As of the writing of this book, the New York State Senate passed a bill (SB6087-A), which would make it possible for churches to worship in public schools. But the New York State Assembly has to pass a corresponding bill (A8800-A), in order for this law to be effective. Then the governor would have to approve. Numerous people have contacted the State Assembly, urging members to sign bill A8800-A.

Many politicians and government officials have stood in unity with faith leaders on this issue. Thousands have come together to march across the Brooklyn Bridge, and to protest the injustice that was committed against the Church. Many have met in lower Manhattan to rally, with some arrested.

The intercession for NY is so critical at this time. If we lose this case, I know that it will be the beginning of the end for the free speech rights of the Church. The Body of Christ needs to continue in a united front against this clear violation of our rights. I know that the marches and protests are a reflection of answered prayers. My only comment here is that *all protests* should be done peaceably and in compliance with the law. This is important so that the enemy has no legal ground to retaliate. Martin Luther King protested peacefully.

I could not support the Occupy Wall Street movement because there were so many violations of the law. But I still believe the Lord allowed that movement to get America's attention.

I again emphasize that before Occupy Wall Street and the NYC Church-ban protests, our ministry had been praying in the exact same area for revival and revolution. Please see the 2011 YouTube videos on our website for proof of the timing of these prayers (visit www.kingdomdominioninternational.com and click "videos"). It is so clear to me that God is answering our prayers. And the entire Church Body has been praying over the years that an unprecedented awakening would hit this land.

Jurisdictional Intercession

After speaking in 2012 with different NYC leaders relating to the recent Church-ban issue, I discovered that many prayer teams had interceded in Albany, near the legislative offices responsible for implementing statutes to permit worship in public schools. In addition, the Lord recently led different prayer teams to strategically intercede in front of government offices in Manhattan, where decisions are made affecting this ban, and in other targeted areas throughout the five boroughs.

The Lord said to me that He had given certain intercessors *jurisdiction* over different areas. In the legal field, the term "jurisdiction" carries much significance. For example, a court does not have authority to render a decision in a case if it lacks jurisdiction. This simply means "an area or range of authority," or "the territory/land covered by this authority."

I remember sharing with one group that I knew the Lord had given me specific authority over certain areas in NYC. For example, before our ministry started renting space in a public school near the Wall Street area (close to the Occupy Wall Street uprising, and near City Hall, where the Church-ban protests erupted), I had a dream about interceding in that "exact location."

God will reveal our assignments through many different avenues, and we must pay close attention and listen for His "timing," which is critical.

I recall sharing a dream with fellow believers in 2002, about a principality in Manhattan (by the way, I believe this demonic force is *the number one spirit* that must come down in order to see breakthrough). I recall taking a group of mature intercessors to prayer-walk against this principality. A few weeks later, one of them developed cancer, and I knew that person had been attacked. I recall that, as we locked arms and prayer-walked, we had all felt this "larger-than-life" force trying to "suck us in."

In March, 2012, right before the publishing of this book, I had a dream about an attack by flood coming against what I believe was NYC, although it may have been NJ. I saw poor and wealthy families in what looked like separate escape vessels, trying to survive the flood. The Lord took me inside a few of these different vessels as the water kept rising and threatening. An angel then lifted me high above a bridge and told me (as the voice did in my 2008 dream), "Speak to this storm so that it can stop."

I believe this was a prophetic dream about a coming catastrophe. The Lord has called me as a watchman on the wall to intercede for NYC and the US. God's ways are not our ways, but over and over in the Bible He answered the cries of intercessors like Moses.

Jesus spoke to the wind and commanded it to cease (Mark 4:39). Elijah prayed down rain (I Kings 18:45). I personally saw the Lord stop storm clouds as I prayed on rainy days in Foley Square.

The key for intercession is to make sure that 1) we have heard from God, 2) we are consecrated for the assignment, 3) we do not move outside of God's timing, and 4) we do not take immature Christians out with us to war against these *high level principalities*. If we do the latter, there are sure to be injuries.

For the unbeliever, the things that I am saying may not be understandable. But for those in the Church Body, especially mature intercessors, we know that Satan is *real* and will retaliate by attacking us in our finances, health and families, *if these principles are not followed.* Anyone can pray to God; but if you are a new believer, I caution you to just ask Jesus to help your city in the areas I outline throughout the book. Do not just start to challenge and bind Satan, especially if there is heavy sin in your life. The enemy *will* fight back.

Again, I emphasize that, as the Church Body, we must support each other as the Lord leads us to pray, and as He reveals a part of the strategy to different intercessors. If I am not led to go out with a team, I most certainly will cover that group in prayer, from a distance. And, *over the last decade or so*, the Lord has already been soaking NYC in fervent, targeted intercession. For example, I know prayer teams over the years have targeted specific blocks throughout the state for intercession.

There is no one *prayer strategy* that holds the single key to revival in the state (although I do believe there are a few *major principalities* which must be defeated in order to see breakthrough). I firmly believe that it will take a *combination* of different teams of anointed intercessors to bring down the many different territorial principalities which hold the people of NYC and the US captive.

I therefore welcome all anointed "prayer movements." Yes, let us arise and let God's enemies be scattered. Let these movements catch fire throughout the land, Lord. In the same way that Occupy Wall Street caught fire, let Your Church come forth. Let the mighty armies of the Lord arise in peaceful fasting, prayer and protest, and overthrow the spiritual forces of darkness that threaten our great country!

I will share in another book several specific jurisdictional areas that the Lord assigned me, and the mistakes I made along the way. Intercession is not something to be taken lightly, and I have personally been injured by going out presumptively against a principality, outside of God's timing. I "stress" that for this *level of intercession*, we *must* be living a holy life, and we *must* hear from God if we step out against these higher level principalities.

I know that the Lord assigned me the Foley Square park area in front of the NY Supreme Court for intercession, especially in light of my legal background.

Let's fight the good fight of faith. We cannot sit back while the enemy advances. We must fight peaceably so that the next generation can live in a land that honors the mighty name of Jesus. We must fight while we still have the freedom to do so.

Years ago, there was public outcry against the University of North Carolina requiring its freshman class to read a book about the Quran. While the course was later changed from a required to an *elective* class, the Church did not stand together as it should have to protest that issue. I have not read the book in question.

I think the Church needs to peacefully lobby and protest the fact that there are little, if any, *Christian* texts utilized by our colleges (many of which were formed initially as Christian universities, as we saw in Chapter 3). Books like this one should be taught in "elective classes," giving students, especially of Christian backgrounds, opportunities to study the history of the United States from a Christian perspective. After all, Evangelicalism is very much a part of our history.

Many forget that the voice of the people counts tremendously in the United States. This is the way our legal and political systems are organized. We are a nation by the people, and for the people. Christians must not sit back in apathy, but must peacefully and actively protest the injustices that are constantly being done against our religious heritage. As I shared previously, if we do nothing, then we will slowly see all Christian values stripped from the culture.

A majority of our college professors are anti-Christian. We must pray for Christian instructors to be hired in our educational institutions. The area of "education" is one of the Seven Mountains of our culture previously discussed.

One of the arguments presented by faith leaders in the University of North Carolina case was that because this college is state-funded and a majority of the US population claim to be Christian, our funds should not support a required course that we do not want our children exposed to. In the alternative, I would say that we lobby for Christian *elective* classes, if other *elective* classes are allowed.

Yes, we have a voice folks; but many have been asleep. God is waking up the sleeping giants — the sleeping warriors who will pray and peaceably protest, until our voices are heard.

We need to file lawsuits and/or contact our Congressmen and others in government when anti-Christ issues arise in the land. We have done nothing over the years as humanists challenged our Christian emblems, mottos, and laws. Some have held the mistaken belief that we cannot speak out as Christians. Others have chosen to just ignore what is happening, without acknowledging or realizing the long-term impact of actions taken against Christianity.

The spirit of anti-Christ has influenced the minds of people year after year to destroy our Christian foundation. If our population is over 80 percent Christian, then 80 percent of the funding for public programs and institutions come from us.

We have a voice, and a very powerful one if used.

Victory in Education and Government Mountain

I want to make an important point here in the Church's favor as we look at the ongoing fight for the soul of America. I previously mentioned that from the time of *Holy Trinity* (1892), where Justice Brewer proved that we are a Christian nation, as recently as in 1931, the *Macintosh* case upheld the conclusion that we are a Christian country. However, I noted that things shifted significantly in the legal system in 1947, with the *Everson* case extending the Establishment Clause to the states. Then in 1962 and 1963 we had the *Engel* and *Abington* cases, respectively, forbidding prayer in public schools.

The Holy Spirit has now revealed to me a truth that I want to share here. In the June, 2011, *Bronx Household* opinion, the majority gave its ruling in violation of the Church's free speech rights, but the court seemed to note in irritation that:

> The Board has by no means been alone in the belief that the Establishment Clause

requires governmental educational institutions to be cautious of harboring or sponsoring religious activities. The Supreme Court's rulings in *Rosenberger*, *Lamb's Chapel*, and *Good News Club deviated from a previously widespread* governmental and judicial perception of the scope of the Establishment Clause's prohibitions.[3]

The New York Second Circuit cited *three cases* above to show that there has been a *deviation* from prior rulings relating to Establishment cases involving religious activities. *I believe that this reflects a victory for the Church.* I noticed that the three cases mentioned in the opinion above were decided between 1993 and 2001.

In the latest of the cases, the US Supreme Court ruled in *Good News Club v. Milford Central School*,[4] that it was unconstitutional for a public school in Milford, New York, to exclude a Christian group for children, from using the premises after school hours to conduct activities such as Christian Bible study, prayer and singing. In *Lamb's Chapel v. Center Moriches Union Free School District*,[5] the US Supreme Court found unconstitutional a school's refusal to allow a church to show a Christian film.

In *Rosenberger v. Rector & Visitors of the University of Virginia*,[6] the US Supreme Court held that the University of Virginia discriminated against a Christian newspaper through its policy of not reimbursing the newspaper for printing expenses.

Of course, the *Bronx Household* court tried its best to distinguish those three cases, noting that none of those activities involved a "service."[7]

My point here is that we need to highlight the victories as well as defeats. There have been many losses, but the 1993 to 2001 *deviation* in case law referenced by the Second Circuit in *Bronx Household* clearly shows that the Church's prayer for a change in the *Mountains of government and education* is being answered.

We must continue to pray, file lawsuits, and peacefully protest wrongs.

As an attorney, I know the significance of the New York Second Circuit negative ruling, which permitted the BOE to ban religious worship in public schools. That holding could set precedent and become another landmark anti-Christian decision in the continual battle of good against evil. It is wonderful to see so many churches finally coming together to fight peaceably. This means war.

First Events in a Century

The number "11" in the Bible represents God's judgment. As mentioned earlier, I noticed during the summer of 20*11* all of the "firsts" in the destructive events that hit the nation. The Lord had me examine all of these, and I noticed over and over that there had been many things occurring for the first time, or for the first time in approximately *one hundred years*.

For example, 1) NYC experienced the tremors from an earthquake for the *first* time in a century, 2) the NYC mayor evacuated the public transportation system for the *first* time ever, 3) the US lost its national credit rating for the *first* time, and 4) there were several other natural disasters where I heard the news describe the events as *firsts* in a century. I will not mention specifically the natural disasters that I discovered with this *century-theme*, out of respect for those who may have suffered losses. Jesus wept over the condition of the city of Jerusalem. In the same way, my heart is heavy over the condition of the nation and world.

I have tried in this book to not *harshly* point out areas that violate God's statutes, yet at the same time relate the message I believe God has given me. In fact, I have pointed the finger significantly on the Church, in an attempt to prove my point that we *are all sinners* and need God's grace.

Why have I taken this approach? My goal is to present the biblical basis for Christianity's position on many issues that are highly controversial in our nation at this time, and give readers an opportunity to form their own conclusions.

I want to focus instead on how we can pray to *avert further catastrophes*. God has called me as an *intercessor to pray for mercy*. The condition of the world right now speaks for itself that something is terribly wrong.

As I looked at all of the record-breaking events (most with 100 years previously as an approximate date of the last similar event), I knew that the Lord was speaking to us. I realized that the "century" theme was significant. The last *national* revival, which started on Azusa Street in California, also occurred approximately 100 years ago.

I then knew that God was about to bring a revival of unprecedented proportions to America and that, just as destruction had hit so many different areas, this awakening would release His mercy throughout the land in an unprecedented manner (with the last similar event having occurred a century ago).

The Church now speaks of this Third Great Awakening or outpouring, which will be known as an Apostolic Reformation. C. Peter Wagner, a leader I greatly admire, is one of the generals at the forefront of this movement. This move seeks to restore the form of the early Church government, including the offices of apostles, as well as to otherwise revolutionize society.

Coming Social Reform

The Third Awakening (which I believe may have already begun) will seek to transform American and world culture in every area for Christ, including business, government, the arts, and religion (see Seven Mountains of culture in Chapter 6). Christians would like to see righteous leaders elected to office, abortion prohibited, and a general transformation of lives to conform to biblical principles. For the past few years, different groups across the land and nations have been praying for revival. I will just highlight some of them from over the last two years.

Several national prayer events occurred in 2010, including "The Call Sacramento," the "MayDay" event in Washington, thousands of "National Day of Prayer" services, and the "Pray and Act" movement, which called for prayer and fasting for a nation in crisis. In 2011, we had the US May 5th "National Day of Prayer," the June 2nd "Global Day of Prayer" (nations around the world gathered to pray for God's healing of their land), and "The Response" on August 6th, where approximately 30,000 gathered in Houston, Texas, to pray for our nation in crisis.

As stated earlier, through "Awaken NYC," our ministry started a prayer and fast movement (skipping one meal a day, initially for 40 days but extended to 90 days) on July 14, 2011, based on the book of Joel. We later found out about the Houston "Response" prayer/fast gathering (August 6th), which was based on that same book of the Bible. I then knew that it was God's Spirit confirming His leading for our event.

The Lord has placed us outside, right in front of the NY Supreme Court in Manhattan, where we have been crying out for repentance and a coming back to God. The Lord has moved powerfully, as noted previously. The place of our meeting is very near to the World Trade Center site and the Wall Street area where our stock market crashed. This is significant because we are located in the financial heartbeat of the US. I know from the dream the Lord gave me in 2008 before the stock market crashed (concerning a tornado heading toward New York City — see Chapter 7 for details) that this event is a Divine appointment.

The Lord has assigned me as a forerunner to pray for God's protection and blessing over America, to warn the people of impending darkness, and to call for repentance. He brought revival to this area in 1857 and is re-digging the old wells. As an apostle, as well as an attorney who has worked in this area extensively over the past several years, I know that He has given me spiritual authority against the forces of darkness binding up the area.

All of the aforementioned prayer events are targeting the world in crisis and seeking to move the hand of the Lord for revival and awakening. This revival will be an awakening because it seeks to transform our very culture, both locally and nationally. This last end-time movement of God will not just be an awakening, but it will be a revolution that will forever change the face of the way we "do Church." Miracles, signs and wonders will be the norm for ministers and lay people alike.

This author is not necessarily in agreement on *all doctrinal views* in the movements of God on the scene as of 2011/2012, but there are some I believe who are being used tremendously by God. And, as in any movement, there are false spirits which will infiltrate and try to corrupt what the Lord is attempting to do. We must pray for discernment and that the Lord separates the wheat from the tare.

As I mentioned, however, there is a true awakening move of God that is about to break forth locally and internationally, with great miracles, signs and wonders to follow. There will be radical changes in the socioeconomic and political arenas of the world. And of course, as with any great movement, there will be critics both inside and outside of the Church who will challenge what God is doing. I believe that there will be unprecedented impact through many great leaders. God's Kingdom will be advanced to prepare for His return, and the gates of hell shall not prevail against it.

I have sat under the ministries of many great men and women of God. The Lord will always establish a great work through chosen vessels. He has mightily used many in past revivals, such as Charles Finney and Kathryn Kuhlman.

If I could name one past revivalist that I admire greatly, it would be Charles Finney. His deep cry for a true heart conversion echoes my cry to God in the wilderness. He also was willing to leave his legal career (the Lord has asked me to do this as well), forsaking all for the gospel.

If I could name one past healing evangelist that I greatly admire, it would be Kathryn Kuhlman. There seems to be so much I have in common with her testimony, such as 1) the lonely path the Lord put me on throughout my life, and some of the things He has asked me to give up, and 2) I once heard her preach that she knew the exact day when she died to self; as I explained in the beginning of the book, the Lord put me in a wilderness period for several years, where He taught me how to die to myself so that I could live in Him.

I came up in Pentecostal denominations under anointed men and women of God, and before I even heard about God anointing folks in this end-time to do great miracles, He had anointed me with the gifts of healing and the prophetic.

The Bible teaches that God (the Holy Spirit gives gifts as He "wills," not as we "will": 1 Cor. 12:11) calls each of us into the office we are to walk in (predestination: Rom. 8:30) before we are born. We then later come into that calling and anointing though trials, personal consecration, and sometimes through impartation — which simply stirs up dormant gifts. In addition, the Bible tells us that in this end-time, God will pour out His Spirit on all flesh, and all in the Body will move in some level of the anointing (especially the prophetic: Joel 2:28), unlike previous times in history.

I will now continue my story of the path that the Lord took me on toward manifesting His true power. Between 2008 and early 2011, He stripped me completely of the healing anointing I had seen evident in the ministry and put me in a dry place so that He could resurrect His glory (Christ glorified) through my life.

I want to emphasize here that I am simply a vessel. I have no power in and of myself: All power belongs to God, and I give Him all glory and honor. I heard one preacher aptly put it that we are simply "hoses" through whom He flows. We dare not touch God's glory. He shares His glory with no man.

So the mantle I now wear, I could never say I received from the impartation of any man. I received it from God Himself. Death to self meant death to my will. I realized that throughout my beginnings in ministry, I had operated mostly in self-effort: this is why the ministry could not grow. I had to put down "my ministry" and pick up God's ministry. As Ms. Kuhlman would say, "I knew the day my ministry ended and God's began." Jesus only did the will of the Father. God then imparted unto me a true apostolic mantle filled with His glory. I can truly say I was commissioned and ordained by the Father.

I therefore also agree wholeheartedly with Kathryn Kuhlman's past statement that the anointing of God *costs us everything*. My acquaintances know that I have sacrificed my own life for the gospel. I have given up everything just to behold the beauty of my Savior. Everyone who has been around me knows that I will stop everything if I believe there is some flesh trying to glorify itself in the Lord's presence. No flesh will be able to lay claim to His glory. We are just vessels.

The Lord revealed to me in a dream an army of young people moving in great power. There will be a huge outpouring among the young people in fulfillment of the prophesy in Joel, that the sons and daughters will be used by God in this end-time. Even the old and those who think their time for ministry has passed will be used mightily. Every believer who is available will be anointed in this time period; no one in the Body of Christ is exempt.

Many marketplace ministries have been released over the past several years as well. The Lord will continue to use people mightily in business and corporate affairs. This will not be "Church as usual," but will be a contagious Holy Ghost fire that will spread to the uttermost parts of the earth, in full proof that Jesus Christ reigns! According to the Bible, in this end-time, the Church will bring in the greatest harvest of souls for the Kingdom.

Revolution and Peaceful Protest Prayer Points

- That the 1947 *Everson* case, which extended the Establishment Clause to states, is reversed

- That the *Bronx Household* wins the new case filed against the NY Board of Education

- That the US Supreme Court continues to uphold *Christian* chaplains leading legislative sessions in prayer

- That all US court cases and statutes which violate biblical precepts be reversed

- That the emblems of Moses and the Ten Commandments remain in the US Supreme Court building and in all public buildings, and are discussed in schools, tours, and other forums, as a part of our religious heritage

- That the courts rule that all remaining Christian mottos, emblems, common law, or customs, *not be removed*, with the holding based not just on *tradition*, but as proof that we *are* a Christian country

- That the anti-Christ spirit be stopped in its tracks as it tries to influence people to stifle the truths of our Christian foundation, all in the name of disestablishment

- That the *Holy Trinity* case is affirmed in its ruling that we are a Christian nation

- Cover the ACLJ and other similar agencies in prayer as they continue to fight against the uprooting of our Christian heritage

- That the American people who call themselves "Christian" are touched deeply by the Holy Spirit and come to a full knowledge and acceptance of Christ as Lord

- That Christian history books such as this one are offered in *elective* college classes

- That a transformation occurs and the Seven Mountains of our culture are won for God: *business, religion, education, government, family, media, arts and entertainment*

- That the Lord raises up some passionate people, *especially the young*, to pray, advocate, and protest aggressively, but peacefully, on these issues

- That awakening, reformation, revolution and prayer movements such as "Awaken NYC," spread across the US and the world

Conclusion

It is overwhelmingly clear from the evidence presented in this book that America was a Christian nation from its foundation, and is still a Christian republic. The entire legal, economic, social and governmental structure in America was influenced by the gospel of Jesus Christ. Although some of our presidents may have been swayed by popular Enlightenment Deist and Masonic beliefs prevalent among the elite of that day, their foundations were based in the Christian faith.

I have presented overwhelming proof that even the US Supreme Court Justices used the Christian religion as a basis for decisions. The Constitution's separation of Church and State clause relates to protecting the right of people to practice whatever religion they choose, but was never meant to exclude what was behind our belief system—namely, Christianity. The Establishment Clause was never meant to extend to the individual states, but should only apply to Congress' (federal government) actions.

Despite the Deist and Masonic influences on a few of the founding fathers, clearly our culture, in terms of values and customs, was based on biblical precepts. We continued with these principles, although slowly losing the right focus over the years. As mentioned earlier, we see a prime example of biblical influence in 1890, when the US Supreme Court ruled against polygamy. These are the same precepts that should continue to guide decisions relating to abortion and Christian prayer in schools.

I believe that enough proof remains in our culture to show that we are still a Christian nation – that enough of the laws, emblems and Christian claims of the people remain, to support this belief. However, we must come to the knowledge that "Separation of Church and State" is not violated by continuing to allow Christian beliefs to govern this republic.

We must be careful that in protecting "freedom," we do not compromise the biblical standards that made this country great. Taking Christian prayer out of schools has done this country a great injustice and was never the spirit of the Constitution. These prayers served to further recognize and ask for Jesus' powerful intervention in our affairs, as Franklin rightly noted concerning the Revolutionary War of the 1700s.

Comparison of Past and Future Awakening Moves

If I could summarize the greatest impact of each of the two past Awakening movements of God, I would say that: 1) the First Awakening of the 1700s continued the Protestant influence of moving away from ceremonial Catholic rituals to an Evangelical-style preaching, with emphasis on a personal relationship with Christ, resulting in a *distinct Evangelical culture* developing in America, fought against pagan Enlightenment influences, and established Christian colleges/education; and 2) the Second Awakening of the 1800s continued to change the face of religion (personal relationship with Christ), continued to challenge Enlightenment paganism, impacted the end of slavery, spread the gospel locally and globally through Christian education and missionary institutions, and continued the development of the American Evangelical culture. The Second Awakening had a much wider geographic and global reach than the first.

Pentecostal and healing movements of God have also shaped our culture since the Second Awakening. The Third Great Awakening (which I believe has already been set in motion, but will begin to explode in the years to come) will by far surpass the prior revivals in many respects: 1) It will continue to change the way America practices its faith, but this time miracles, signs and wonders will become the norm in the Church Body (Joel 2's promise of the outpouring of the Spirit); 2) It will result in a great transference of wealth into the hands of the entire Church Body; 3) It will continue to challenge the intellectualism and humanism now present in our society (residue of Enlightenment ideologies); and 4) It will have a far greater global impact than the first two as it transforms the Seven Mountains of US and world culture for Christ.

This nation must turn back to God. How do we turn back? By repenting for our past sins, even dating back to root anti-Christian influences. How do we turn back? By ensuring that true Christian values permeate every sphere of our culture — from legal to business to government to the arts and entertainment.

For those who argue that it's hopeless because paganism had already infiltrated from the beginning, I point to the awakening fires that have already burned throughout America to stir our consciousness back to God.

Unfortunately, these periods of revival will often die down, and pagan values will again creep in. *We need a revolution.* We need a radical transformation that will not just last for a decade or two, but will come and stay for good. It is the only way we will win the war against the enemy and keep the victory in the long run. If we implement and keep our Christian values, then God will keep America great; if we digress and move back to pagan influences, we will lose the war.

In 2011, I heard a passionate appeal by a young man during the Occupy Wall Street march. He stated that if we lose America, we lose the only nation in the world where there is true freedom and opportunity. This is indeed a unique nation, where we are free to practice our religious beliefs without persecution, and where we can start with nothing and yet still become successful.

Let us do everything we can to maintain the heritage that we still have, and to reclaim what we have lost.

We must earnestly pray that the Christian values we still possess remain. We looked earlier at the legal principle of "original intent." Keeping Christian values and traditions in place is not the same as "religious control," which the first settlers wanted to guard against. Atheists and humanists have methodically misinterpreted the original intent of the forefathers as they attempt to strip America little by little of its Christian birthright.

Now churches in New York state are engulfed in a legal battle to protect our freedom of speech rights in renting public space. When we look at the reasoning in some of these cases, it is clear that the courts could easily rule one way or the other. Only prayer and the hand of God can change things. We see the results of prayer when we look at cases such as *Good News Club*, *Lamb's Chapel* and *Rosenberger*, which the *Bronx Household* court noted *deviated* from prior rulings. These cases have been decided in the Church's favor.

I remind atheists and humanists here of our first president's warning noted earlier that, despite pride in intellectualism, we must not conclude that we can maintain morality in society *without religion.*

As much as we may want to argue to the contrary, the evidence is clear that we trusted Jesus from the very beginning, and we must trust Him now to save our country. Will you join us in this spiritual war for the soul of America?

Notes

1. *The Bronx Household of Faith v. Board of Education of the City of New York*, No. 07-5291-cv (2d Cir. June 2, 2011) 10, 11, 24 (Emphasis added).
2. *Ibid.,* at 24.
3. *Ibid.,* at 26.
4. *Good News Club v. Milford Central School*, 533 U.S. 98 (2001).
5. *Lamb's Chapel v. Center Moriches Union Free School District*, 508 U.S. 384 (1993).
6. *Rosenberger v. Rector & Visitors of the University of Virginia*, 515 U.S. 819 (1995).
7. *Bronx Household* at 11.

Study Notes

Study Notes

Salvation

If you do not know Jesus Christ as Lord and Savior, please repeat the following prayer out loud:

Father God, I come to you a sinner. I repent from all of my sins, known and unknown. Forgive me Lord, for all of the ways I have transgressed against You. I thank You for the blood of Your Son Jesus, which was shed for me on the cross. I believe that Jesus Christ is Lord. I confess with my mouth and believe in my heart that He rose from the dead. Therefore, Your word says I am born again, and my sins are thrown into the sea of forgetfulness. Come into my heart Lord Jesus and change my life. I ask that You heal me now physically, emotionally and spiritually.

That is it. You are now accepted into the Beloved. It's all by faith, not by any goodness of our own. All have sinned and fallen short of the glory of God. Find a Bible believing church near you. Welcome to the family! Please visit our ministry website noted below, and sign in on our guestbook if you need help finding a church home. Or you can write to:

KDI Ministries, 110 Wall Street, 11th Floor, New York, NY 10005-3817

www.kingdomdominioninternational.com
or e-mail
info@kingdomdominioninternational.com

Disclaimer: *Please note that fasting should be done by believers in Jesus Christ, and after consulting with a local Church Body. Prayer must be coupled with fasting in order to see results. Each person must consult with his or her physician before fasting, and be led by God in this endeavor. If you are interested in learning more, or standing with us in this fast and prayer movement, please e-mail us or sign in on our ministry website as noted below, and click "Guestbook."*

www.kingdomdominioninternational.com
or e-mail
info@kingdomdominioninternational.com

You can follow the church's prayer movement on social media at:

twitter.com/KingdomDomi

http://www.AwakeningNYC.blogspot.com

ABOUT THE AUTHOR

Dr. Michelle A. Morrison is of Jamaican descent but grew up in the United States. She is the Sr. Apostle of Kingdom Dominion International Ministries, a multi-cultural church located in downtown New York City. Dr. Morrison graduated from Columbia University with a BA in English, and from Georgetown University Law with her Juris Doctorate. She also carries her Masters and Doctorate in the ministry.

Dr. Morrison is the CEO of several organizations, including YesUCan! Community and Economic Development Corporation (YUC!), a social enterprise. The mission of YUC! is to bring financial freedom to the poor cross-culturally. She realizes that during this recession, "poverty has no race," and that so many are in dire need — as evidenced by the Occupy Wall Street uprising. Thus, she is a social entrepreneur. YUC! is a grass-roots organization that seeks to connect the unemployed with job and business resources, as well as to implement other initiatives such as low income housing.

Although a NYC attorney at law, Dr. Morrison advocates primarily the cause of the gospel – the life, death and resurrection of Jesus Christ.

She has the fire of Elijah and the warrior call of Deborah to tear down the strongholds of the enemy and re-build the old waste places. Dr. Morrison is commissioned as a forerunner to "prepare the way of the Lord," and serve as one of the catalysts for the end-time Third Awakening. She is anointed for miracles, signs and wonders, and to fulfill the great commission of spreading the gospel to the uttermost parts of the earth.

If you are interested in making a financial contribution toward the vision of YUC!, please visit our website at www.yesuc.org and click on the "donate" link, or write to PO Box 981, New York, N.Y. 10008-0981.